my cool® treehouse.

my cool® treehouse.

an inspirational guide to stylish treehouses

jane field-lewis

PAVILION

contents

introduction

Beloved for centuries as ramshackle palaces of backyard escape and fun, the modern-day treehouse has evolved from its more traditional forebears, in the process morphing and expanding its agenda to capture the heart and soul of a new breed of acolytes. Versatile and endlessly adapting, it gives us a unique opportunity for creative expression as well as an individualistic challenge. It enables us to build on 'unbuildable' plots, create unusual business models and even use it as a form for art installations. What has stayed the same, however, and true to the pioneers of this architectural genre, is the innate spirit of adventure and freedom that has always been the terrain of the treehouse builder. The only pages still remaining from the old rule book are the ones relating to physics. The rest are open and up for reinvention.

Unfortunately, I don't own a treehouse, but I still love them and identify with the souls who do. Although we were generally well-behaved, the long school summer holidays, especially during harvest-time, gave us children the opportunity to let rip. We used to annoy the local farmers who travelled up the flinty lane that ran along the back of our house. Collecting hay bales from the fields, we would create an impromptu barricade in the lane, climb a nearby tree and wait for the kick-off. Somehow, up that tree we found sanctuary and we weren't scared of the tirade of justified abuse coming our way; we enjoyed it, stifling our laughter, the memories of our impervious irresponsibility still making me giggle today.

It strikes me that a treehouse does just that. It creates its own world, its own atmosphere. It's a distillation of some of the values and qualities we cherish most: resourcefulness, shelter, safety, exploration and romance, all entwined with an innate childlike desire for inhabiting something that is out of reach – a cabin in the trees or a simple sturdy branch will suffice.

Literature, too, understands this principle. Magical tales are spun by Enid Blyton of her faraway trees while Tolkien's elf houses and Roald Dahl's *The Minpins* unashamedly take delight in harnessing the imaginative power of the treehouse. The satisfaction of leaving all your worldly worries behind as you climb up into the sanctuary of a tree is still very seductive. Perhaps it's this other-worldly sensation that grabs us as children and never leaves us even as we make the transition to adults.

Often constructed from entirely found and recycled materials, these amazing buildings are sometimes created minimally but always sensitively and joyfully. The Swiss Family Robinson's fantastical treehouse has a modern resonance: both Robinson Crusoe and the Swiss Family recycled the wreckage of their boat to build a refuge – a delicious dose of self-reliance and resourcefulness. Using available materials is fundamental to each story, and even though nowadays we may not have the hull of a shipwreck to hand we can still make do with the discarded wood, window frames, doors and cladding that have been scavenged from the waves of modern life, and can weave them into our own treehouse builds.

I hope that this book will illuminate the myriad possibilities of elevating yourself off the ground and creating a shelter high up in the air or just embracing the spirit of a treehouse in the design. In some way, with a soupçon of resourcefulness and imagination, each and every one of us can experience our own version of arboreal paradise. The spirit of these creators is for the sharing.

Embracing a truly worldwide approach, this book finds inspiration from far and wide: from contemporary minimalist treehouses, recycled urban structures in backyards, bespoke Welsh hideaways and glass walls in the African wilderness to cabins perched in trees in the scented lavender fields of southern Italy. Creativity and vision definitely anchor each and every one of them firmly to the ground.

Enjoy!

simple

These simple structures take us back to basics and what a treehouse means and symbolises for many of us. There's something magical and liberating about climbing a tree and leaving the terrestrial world behind – life slows down and it rekindles the spirit of the child within us. The charming treehouses featured in this chapter resonate with the love of a parent who wants to create a unique experience for their children, which will stay with them forever and capture the Swiss Family Robinson spirit. And there's no reason why 'simple' should be construed as deficient; on the contrary, ideas and vision lead the way. John Beard used his experience of set design to create a magical inner-city London treehouse for his children, while Nicko Björn Elliott involved his children at every stage of the design process while constructing his Toronto treehouse.

The treehouse, in its most simple and fundamental form, enables us to escape from the everyday pressures of modern life and feel closer to nature. The Tree Room in Canada, designed by an architect for his family, exhibits the finest distilled, minimal treehouse design ever – the walls are half removed, the windows frameless and glassless, blurring the boundaries and loosening the walls between a man-made structure and the surrounding arboreal world.

Best of all, to construct a really simple treehouse, specialist skills are not always necessary. The DIY treehouse is achievable and buildable by even the most DIY-phobic among us, and it can be erected quickly without using any tools at all. The Canopy Staircase edits the process and experience right down to the bare essentials; it's the branches and tree canopy themselves that provide the treehouse experience. To enjoy this feeling of immortality and look down on humdrum daily existence from a bird's eye view, all you need is the means to get yourself up there into the unspoiled foliage.

diy treehouse

Rogier Martens and Sam van Veluw of the design company Aandeboom, which is based in Utrecht in the Netherlands, have created the DIY (do-it-yourself) treehouse, distilling both the structure and the essence of what constitutes a treehouse down to its simplest form. Even a novice could assemble it, provided they had the skill set to be reasonably competent at building flat-pack furniture. The pieces just slot together and fasten to a tree, without damaging it, by means of two ratchet straps.

The treehouse, which measures just 120cm x 120cm x 115cm (4ft x 4ft x 3ft 9in), is constructed from water-resistant plywood and can be built in 30 minutes without any glue or screws. Designed to be a temporary structure, the flat-pack contains just seven pieces and, of course, a step-by-step manual. All you have to do is to source a suitable tree. The designers describe their DIY treehouse as 'a boy's dream comes within reach', as it is universal and accessible to everyone.

style notes

Although modest, unfussy and raised just a few feet off the ground, this idiosyncratic structure is enough to create the treehouse experience – a sense of freedom and escape. Indeed, its simplicity opens up infinite possibilities, giving it a slightly magical quality. There is something extraordinary and almost subversive about it and empowering. All

you need do is pick your spot and, suddenly, 'I think I'll have my tree house right here' becomes totally feasible – it's so liberating. And, rather uniquely, it's all about you, the owner and treehouse inhabitant, conveying a sense of destination rather than taking possession of a specified piece of space.

Unlike fixed structures, this unique treehouse can change both its perspective and outlook. Hence, you can pivot on the same tree, choose a different aspect, follow the sun around or even select a completely different location. Witty, playful and with a light touch, this collapsible flat-pack can be folded away and disappear. Just like the memory of a childhood refuge, it somehow embodies this idea.

It almost resembles a bird's nest, pinned onto a suitable configuration of branches at a certain height. You can use any easily accessible structure as long as it provides a platform on which you can build. The treehouse is a temporal structure – a public space that can be inhabited and owned momentarily. And although it's fleeting and impermanent, it can still be treasured.

This treehouse is a satisfyingly simple build, the pieces slotting together like an elementary jigsaw. The only extraneous feature is the protruding peg-style bracket on the front apex. A perch for a bird perhaps? Or a coat or a bag? Whatever it may be, it's a delightful invitation to something or someone.

Architect Nicko Björn Elliott of the Brooklyn-based practice Civilian Projects relishes different materials and forms. He believes in observing the details and doing his best to provide creative and thought-provoking solutions. When a project to design a backyard children's play treehouse in Toronto came his way, it was a joyous opportunity, working with clients who really appreciated good design. They wanted to include their children, aged 10 and 8 years, in the collaborative design process, making them feel engaged and valued as important participants in determining the outcome.

Communication was key and to convey his ideas and explain the methods of larger-scale architecture to his clients, Nicko made a 3D model of how he envisaged the build. Together, they set about creating an energetic space using unconventional materials, including some discontinued heavy-duty corrugated fibreglass, which they managed to procure for a good price. It wasn't ideal but it had some amazing characteristics and was incredibly robust. Slotted securely into a spruce frame and sealed off with thin coloured slats, it proffered structural and translucent qualities. With the colours chosen by the children, this unique approach adds huge visual advantages. Everything becomes diffused and the colours are transmitted through to the skin of the treehouse. Under the branches, the treehouse is supported by timber pillars. A ladder provides access upwards while a fireman-style pole points in the direction back down to ground level – a quicker journey down than up.

modern backyard treehouse

style notes

Sturdy and luminous, this translucent coloured treehouse was designed as the perfect garden playhouse, an escape into the imagination. Both visually and literally fun, it is a changing sculptural shape. Movement and speed are encouraged by the design, the children's shadows dancing through the space as they clamber up the ladder and then whizz at speed back down the pole to earth.

Unusually, with its choice of colours and materials, this building is equally enjoyable inside and out. The painted slats chosen by the children delicately draw your eye to the colours that permeate the fibreglass. The world outside is blurred, but the crisp lines of the tree, the wood and the frame make the magical world inside an ever-changing prism of colour. Light and colour ripple across the surfaces and refract through the fibreglass, creating the illusion that this structure has been given a cloak of invisibility. It's almost on the verge of disappearing as the sky, shadows, leaves and branches reflect and refract, permeating the structure.

Note the slightly raised pathway below the tree – a thoughtful architectural addition that provides a striking visual link between the ground and the treehouse. Thoroughly modern, striking and simple, this is a valuable lesson in how to use unconventional materials and the available light. It is a backyard play space on stilts and is not only beautiful but also inspiring, where your dreams and imagination can run free.

primrose hill treehouse

For John Beard, a successful film production designer, this backyard urban treehouse in Primrose Hill, north London, represents a simpler but no less thoughtful distillation of his talents. He built it for his children, wanting to make the most of the available space in the garden of his 1850s terraced home. As he says: 'The treehouse didn't take up any space and I wanted to create something out of nothing'. Its scale was determined by a desire not to upset his neighbours whereas his objective was to 'give my kids the sort of adventure they might have if they were lucky enough to have a big garden in the country'.

Home to this treehouse is a hawthorn tree, and John set about the design and construction in much the same way as he would tackle one of his film projects. He describes himself as someone who 'looks at everything everywhere', mentally cataloguing and remembering all the tiniest details and taking in everything he sees.

He sketched the structure and, using familiar building techniques, he constructed a 70cm x 1.30m (2ft 3in x 4ft 3in) frame out of new 10cm x 5cm (4in x 2in) timbers, adding a solid base and back wall. This was bolted to the tree with additional supports beneath. The side and front walls were fashioned out of rough-finished timber and set in a decorative pattern. Several bird nest boxes were fitted to the exterior back face of the treehouse. The doorway was left open and a window opening added on each side. An old tin bucket on a length of sash cord fixed to a roofline pulley keeps the children supplied with their whims, whether they're ice cubes, lemonade or cookies, while the interior has two simple bench seats and a fold-down table.

style notes

For this project John tapped into his incredible memory of things that had caught his attention over the years. His inspiration and final approach was a hybrid design, hailing from a mixture of sources, including Victorian decoratively wood-clad summerhouses, prairie log cabins, and even the mini Swiss chalet style of Eastern European allotment sheds where creative efforts are directed into making something that will benefit all the family, even on a very small patch of agricultural and recreational space.

To achieve this, John needed to choose his materials carefully. In this treehouse with the simplest of forms, it's the basic outline, proportions and visible materials that tell the story. The timber offcuts came from an out-of-town sawmill. What John was after were the exterior bark slices and although, over the years, the bark has fallen off, the grainy wood now has a naturally weathered look. The ladder, also made of sawmill offcuts, has cross-section lengths of smaller-diameter branches, and even though it has become necessary to replace them over the years, a similar wood has been used in the same fashion.

This treehouse enchants not only John's family but also the inhabitants of the canal boats cruising past and the pedestrians, runners and cyclists who use the adjacent towpath as a pleasant alternative to the main road. They all glance up at the treehouse, their attention caught by its engaging structure, and many of them stop to take a photograph of it. Probably, without consciously thinking about it, they somehow understand the simple joy of this most basic but thoughtful building and want to capture and share it with others.

the tree room

Sometimes the ground speaks and geography, the landscape and nature herself call for your attention, presenting ideas and steering your thoughts in a specific direction. This happened to the Canadian architect Christopher Smith on an area of his land called the 'hog's back', a high ledge along a rocky outcrop rising from a 40-hectare (100-acre) field. It's dominated by three prominent pine trees and the overall effect was so dramatic that Christopher wanted to engage with it more fully and create something special and more permanent.

There was already a rudimentary treehouse platform, rough and constructed out of boards about 50cm (1ft 8in) off the ground. Christopher drew up plans to replace this with something altogether more refined, elegant and considered. Building a regular treehouse held no appeal for him – he wanted to reinterpret the traditional model and create something fresh that wasn't a stereotype of a building in a tree. He believes a treehouse doesn't have to be conventional and that suspending a structure is liberating with the feeling of limitless possibility.

His preference was for a more minimal approach, and his challenge was how to inhabit the space with as little of the built environment as possible while not overpowering the trees. To achieve these ends he built the structure in his spare time, piece by piece, in an organic process, requesting and cajoling assistance as and when he needed it and twisting the arms of friends to help provide the strength to hoist it up into place. Made of spruce framing timber and held to the tree by metal buckles, the treehouse moves gently in the wind.

style notes

Just a short walk from Christopher's house, this unique treehouse is quiet, contained, delicate and elegant. It has been designed with vertically spaced wooden struts – there are no solid walls and only the most minimal gestures towards conventional form. The result is a contemplative and meditative space. By reducing the concept of walls, windows and doors down to their simplest form and then removing their solidity, this sketchy yet precise outline forms a definable whole.

The treehouse is raised 4m (13ft) off the ground, and it's reached by a vertical spruce ladder tucked away into a corner at ground level, while another 2.5m (8ft) above the first floor is the even higher open-roofed balcony level with spectacular views of the surrounding countryside. The two floors have a similar 13sq m (140sq ft) footprint. Unusually, form and space – both actual and negative – dictate the available area rather than the materials used.

The fact that the treehouse is as much there as it's not there is a masterclass in minimalism. There is just enough of everything for the space to work effectively: just enough wall, just enough window, just enough... The extraordinary structure looks as if it has been slotted into the forest, lowered from above, like a comb into the trees, the view partially veiled and partly clear. Consequently, it feels and looks grand, despite its neatly compact structure, hovering within the trees, majestic within its terrain.

The creative process occurs in different ways. Some people are inspired by the work of others; some develop an average idea into a great one; and some have a eureka moment. However, others, myself included, need a touch of boredom as a catalyst to spark the magic. As Dorothy Parker said: 'The cure for boredom is curiosity. There is no cure for curiosity.' And that's how this project started. The simple act of climbing a tree made an idea real.

For the designers Thor ter Kulve and Robert McIntyre, that moment occurred on holiday in the Azores. A high stone wall obscured their sea view, so they climbed a tree and an idea struck them: why not design a simple staircase rising up into the canopy? Gradually, by a process of tinkering and problem solving, their brainwave became a reality. In capturing the essence of tree climbing, the branches themselves became an existential treehouse.

Their design for the canopy staircase is no humble ladder but a highly crafted, tree-friendly spiral. The combination of staircase and tree create a circular symbiosis of man, design, craft and wood. Although seemingly simple, the design process was complex. How to create a spiral staircase when the tree is not perfectly straight? And with an uneven surface? And the varying structural strengths of trees? And without harming the trunk? What's even more amazing is that this 7m (22ft) high staircase was assembled without any tools – just a ratchet strap – by only two people in three hours, and it can be taken down in the space of 30 minutes.

canopy staircase

style notes

There is something magical about leaving the security of being at ground level and the stairs resonate as you feel the power of your ascent. Most of us don't experience this feeling once we move beyond childhood. This is a book about treehouses and so it might appear strange that there isn't a physical structure with the usual floor and roof in this story. But the inspiration and value offered by a treehouse can exist without an actual structure built among the branches. By adding obvious elements such as a floor, roof and walls, you enhance the way in which the space can be used, but for the experience and freedom that come with climbing a tree – it's all here.

In its form, the sculptural aerospace feel of this installation and the graphic imprint of the black threads that encircle the trunk and form a rail create a structure that is visually striking and tactile. It is complex yet simple, beautiful and elemental, up close and from a distance.

Their choice of materials was carefully considered. Thick neoprene pads were mounted on sand-cast aluminium joints at each corner to create three soft contact points with the tree. Ash poles attached to the end of each step were strung together with lengths of flexible plastic to create a balustrade with plastic water pipes used as a handrail. Furthermore, the attention was in the detail: each tread of the staircase not only has a coarse top surface for better grip but also its slight curve acts to 'cradle' your foot, increasing the sense of security.

architectural

Challenging terrain, lack of space and the cost of land are all familiar issues for today's architects. When the solution to these challenges isn't staring you in the face, it forces some creative thinking on your part: just how to create something beautiful and functional out of not very much. Not surprisingly, there is a renewed interest in small space design, the ability to imbue even the most modest project with good design and exciting, innovative and courageous thinking. Treehouses are no exception and in the following pages we look at how some talented people have responded to an array of challenges.

From a very glamorous LA treehouse on a tiny slither of back garden to a family treehouse home in Seattle on a steeply rising and wooded plot that most people considered totally unsuitable for building on, we feature some inspirational arboreal builds that have risen to the challenge and created amazing spaces above ground level in built-up urban environments where space is at a premium. On the other side of the world in Vietnam, there's a bamboo house built on stilts that is able not only to withstand seasonal winds and floodwater but is also an affordable and sustainable housing solution.

And there are the young architecture students at Yale who built a skeletal angular treehouse as a community project. This sculptural yet loosely inhabitable space invites visitors to engage with nature and relive their childhood dreams. Finally, there's what might be the world's oldest treehouse – a timeless architectural gem dating from the seventeenth century which is elegant, symmetrical and embodies the finest craftsmanship of Tudor England. Each of these examples is an inspiration, both technically and imaginatively. Their architectural values have not been compromised...not one tiny bit.

blooming bamboo home

This example of a successful combination of thoughtful design and choice of materials is inspiring, both for the small space builder and in the wider context of creating a structure that is totally suited to its specific local environment. In an effort to find a sustainable and affordable housing solution and community facilities that could withstand floods and natural disasters, H&P, a Vietnamese architectural practice, designed this practical yet beautiful bamboo house. Elevated on stilts, it's sturdy enough to withstand not only strong winds but also a 1.5m (5ft) flood, and it's the prototype for many more homes in vulnerable low-lying areas.

Using a fixed frame clad with lengths of bamboo, bamboo wattle, fibreboard and coconut leaf, this house was conceived to be constructed either by mass production or built individually using locally available materials, thereby creating a different look and style, depending on the region. The area beneath the stilts can accommodate floodwater during Vietnam's rainy season while serving at other times as a convenient place to keep animals or plants. The house itself is designed in modular sections, allowing pivoting and the opening and closing of the deck, shutters, doors, windows and verandahs.

The selection of materials used throughout is minimal; principally, narrow-stemmed slats of bamboo form the walls, floor and roof of the house, while the external vertical gardens can be established using larger-diameter sections of bamboo. The construction is achieved by connecting the modular sections via bolting and binding and hanging them together.

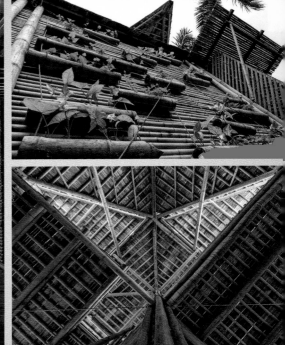

style notes

Although not strictly a treehouse, this is treehouse inspiration in spades – a great example of how to use local materials and a simple, functional design to produce an attractive interior and exterior. The carefully woven house is robust, affordable and truly ecological.

The mesh of bamboo creates a delicate and beautiful surface, a criss-crossing of bars, each with its own natural patina. Another woven dimension is added by the bamboo poles combing the filtered light. The bars of light and shadow ripple across the rich interlocking surface within – akin to being inside a pencil drawing of hatched lines or a huge loom. At night, the house glows and resembles a woven lantern, suspended in the night sky. The roof and wall sections are used as natural ventilation while creating a flexible space. The attic windows open up to the horizontal on each side like an origami paper fortune-teller.

Externally, the vertical garden is a playful and beautiful touch. The large-diameter bamboo poles are set horizontally and hollowed out to act as plant containers along the sides of the building. This is yet another example of resourceful and skilful architecture. Its informing architectural principles could equally apply to a treehouse built in any locale: practicality, affordability and the use of local materials and forms. And it's designed to contend with the elements, too. This innovative space is precise and thoughtfully constructed to serve the spiritual, domestic and even the educational needs of the community.

LA modern

Elegantly textured and angular, this sculptural, cedar-clad, steel and concrete treehouse serves as an office-studio and back garden getaway. It is rich in design quality as well as its structural and finishing materials. A gift from a loving husband to his wife, it rises 3.6m (12ft) from the ground in the backyard of a Los Angeles home. Its owner wanted a grown-up contemporary space that embodied the essence and spirit of the treehouses of her childhood.

However, the perfect structural tree was not an option, so a living tree that had fallen over was used as a reference point and the house, supported by steel columns, appears to rise from it, representing the fragile and respectful relationship between the built and the natural. The hatch opening in the floor serves as a viewing port, presenting a modern take on a traditional treehouse. Similarly, rather than the usual ladder, access is via a cast-concrete staircase. An outdoor shower is cast out of the same material, reinforcing the link with the exterior world – an escape from the internal. Access is via an open metal and wooden plank staircase.

The site is quite small and awkward. To comply with planning requirements the designers, Rockefeller Partner Architects, used angled steel columns for the main structure and to support the roof and floor, achieving a dynamic form that echoes the branches of a real tree. Glazed clerestory windows, sited between the main body of the building and the titanium zinc roof, give the impression that the angular steel-clad butterfly roof is a separate structure. Carefully placed, large-paned and extending from floor to ceiling, they flood the interior with light and their mahogany frames establish a connection with the natural world outside.

style notes

Beyond the scope of usual backyard construction, this unique treehouse has been thought out in an impromptu fashion and built with improvised materials and techniques. A polished piece of design, it is not only conceptually sound and immaculately constructed but also encapsulates the essence of what a treehouse 'is', 'does' and represents to us.

Smooth spherical silver beams lean and tilt like tree trunks from which you might fashion a temporary shelter. The oiled wooden surfaces, both inside and out, are warm, rich and smooth, while the plentiful glazed areas – doors, windows, panels and viewpoints – define this as a space whose purpose is to free the spirit and connect with nature. Set against this, the solid, dignified and substantial creamy-grey cast-concrete staircase, outdoor shower and terracing aid the juxtaposition of lush green grass and the understated wood and metal surfaces.

Despite the exterior high-spec architectural build, the interior has the look and feel of an incredibly personal space – photographs, pictures and a variety of objects are clustered on the shelves between two beams. There is a desk at one end and a daybed with running water and a stove, adding to the sense of respite, inspiration and creativity.

This walnut-panelled and floored structure was conceived as a retreat and a thoughtful place in which to work without unnecessary frills or decorations. Beautifully laid out, it is a treehouse with a view, snug and cosy yet fresh and luminous. Understated luxury is an over-used term but here, in this context, it's absolutely true.

Striking, elegant and simple, the Lau Treehouse was designed, built and funded with the involvement of the widest community. For Griffin Collier and his fellow architecture students at Yale, a discussion of childhood treehouses inspired the creation of a very modern one. When they approached John Loge, the dean, about building a Yale treehouse, he said: 'I don't know but there's no reason not to try and see how far you can get'.

There were obstacles along the way: their initial tree choice proved unsuitable; their design brought its own challenges; and funding the project needed addressing. Not defeated, they pushed ahead and the team grew, targeting an area of land owned by the School of Forestry. As Griffin points out, 'A lot of people don't know that Yale has these forest lands, and a treehouse might be a way to draw attention to them and connect with a greater portion of the community'. A suitable 200-year-old sugar maple on a wooded slope leading down to a brook was identified as a good site, and a Kickstarter appeal raised the necessary funds.

The treehouse was designed to provide a unique perspective from which to observe and experience the natural world. It's an ecocentric design conceived to have minimal impact on the tree while providing an open-sided and roofed structure that connects with the environment at large, including the tree canopy. The wider Yale community pitched in, providing an amalgam of knowledgeable and skilled talent. They included structural engineers and welders who donated their services free of charge. The project grew and took its name from its major

the lau treehouse
benefactors, Claire Woo and Gordon Lau.

style notes

This visually balanced structure stands happily in the forest. Its 'walls' have disappeared and the gently reflective aluminium surface suggests beams of light falling through the trees. For inspiration, Griffin looked beyond architecture to the idea of a geometric treehouse. Simplicity was essential as well as the need to create a space that would not draw attention to itself. The angles of the framework engage with the tree branches as if nature herself was involved in this creation, but this seemingly organic structure is actually two perfect cubes that open up in different directions. One points you up to the canopy while the other hinges downwards into the depths of the forest. Geometry was a guiding force for Griffin, who wanted to create something formal but balanced – two cubes as opposed to 'a crazy spiral' or organic mass.

The treehouse appears to be enmeshed in the trees, sprouting from the branches and giving the sense that the tree has grown around it and lifted it up off the ground like a spindly angular nest. It does not impede or break up the forest in any way. Clearly, it has a graphic quality, which draws inspiration from the interlacing branches.

You leave the leafy ground by a metal-framed, wooden-runged ladder, whose burnished names are testimony to the energy, time and resourcefulness of everyone who contributed. The structure is designed to move with the wind as well as the girth of the tree. Complex and balanced from every angle, it is a deceptively simple design which, in its development and distillation, reminds us of the sense of achievement that ideas and perseverance can bring.

treehouse home

Many of us dream of building our own home, but if we want to build in a large urban metropolis the excitement swiftly wanes, defeated by cost and poor supply of land. Here in Seattle is an example of folk who weren't discouraged. Discovering an 'un-buildable' plot on an inaccessible, steep 50-degree slope, with no mains services and 6m (20ft) beyond the accessible roadway, the architect Prentis Hale didn't instantly discount its potential. Relishing the properties of this unique site, he set about creating a family home high up within the tree canopy. His plan was to build a cost- and resource-efficient building, utilising the location, view, light and space to accentuate the experience of arboreal living. This process was not going to be a quick fix and it took 10 years of planning, design and construction before the treehouse was realised.

The keys to the design decisions were determined by making the best use of the available natural light and space. Rather than using costly materials, he looked for inexpensive products and finishes. Building on a steep slope required geological testing to confirm its suitability to support the 11 auger cast piles that would anchor the structure. Supported by a steel framework, the wood-framed treehouse eventually emerged, cantilevered and elegant.

The floor plan was kept simple with skylights and metal-framed large windows connecting the house to the treescape while a double-height section made the interior feel larger and more airy. In keeping with the ecological nature of the site, the treehouse is 'green' – a thermally efficient envelope with a heat recovery system in which the skylight passively cools and ventilates the house and the water is heated by solar tanks.

style notes

This is a beautiful structure on a complicated plot – luminous and airy. In a tonal mixture for the exterior cladding, multi-toned roofing asphalt is laid in panels, evoking the free-form natural bark camouflage and enabling the house to blend and almost disappear into the dappled backdrop of sky and leaves.

The interior layout was decided by creating a series of cardboard models of the space, including the central skylight. Prentis was interested in Japanese architecture and was inspired by the work of Atelier Bow Wow and Tezuka as well as early Corbusier houses, Ray Kappe's Californian treetop home, Glenn Murcutt's designs and a fantastic build by the Norwegian architect Terje Moe. For the interior surface finish, he used a limited palette of materials and colours – cork for the floors, white walls, dry-wall ceilings and glass – to provide a blank canvas for artworks and objects. His love of plywood shines through with a mixture of pieces designed and built by family and friends, along with vintage and repurposed finds. Across the three floors of the house, the living room forms a multi-functional space with the dining table also serving as a workspace and the sofa as a library with a built-in bookshelf base. Open platform spaces are not what they seem, but with simple lofting round drilled handles they reveal hidden storage areas.

Throughout, the feel is light and natural toned. For example, there's a white, simple IKEA kitchen, handmade furniture, plywood solid shapes inspired by Donald Judd and block colour in the style of Rietfelt. Human endeavour, courage, the persistence of this family and the simple beauty of nature have each played their part in making this amazing treehouse home a reality. Life is on show here: it isn't a precious space but all about family life and spending time together – it has to be practical.

Drive down a winding country lane in deepest rural England and, round a bend in the road, a clutch of what were once agricultural labourers' cottages and the shockingly beautiful and inspiring Grade I listed Pitchford Hall come into view. Within the grounds of one of England's finest Elizabethan houses stands what is thought to be the world's oldest treehouse. Its first recorded mention was in 1692 and it was renovated in 1760 and again in 1980. Sitting in and between the branches of an ancient large-leaved lime tree, it echoes the half-timbered style of the main house and is braced by sturdy steel props.

The hall derives its name from the 'pitch', or bitumen, from its well that was used for protecting and waterproofing the exposed timbers. In 1832, the 13-year-old Princess Victoria (later Queen Victoria) was a guest. She described in her diary 'a curious looking but very comfortable house. It is striped black and white and in the shape of a cottage'. She made use of the treehouse during her visit, climbing into it to watch the local hunt.

The treehouse is a simple squared-off building with a part-glazed door. Each face of the exterior has a single Gothic-shaped window, and the interior has a stripped oak floor and a carved moulded cornice ceiling. The current owners of Pitchford Hall do not provide public access to the treehouse, but it can be viewed from a nearby cottage – Tree House Barn.

tudor
treehouse

style notes

A survivor for more than three centuries, this attractive half-timbered structure feels untouched by the passing of time. The wheat fields, the lowing of the cattle, the birds in full song among the trees – it seems as if this spot has not changed since the treehouse was first built. It sits on a raised area of land, looking down across the neighbouring fields.

This is no ramshackle rustic retreat; it's an elegant, condensed architectural building in a tree. It mirrors the style of the grand hall and even its detailing is considered – the delicate arch of each window, its peak lining up with the central vertical line of the Elizabethan half-timbering; the diagonal beams perfectly symmetrical; and the turned oak finials at the base of the strong corner posts of the structure. The whitewashed wattle between the dark beams creates the graphic geometric that is characteristic of Elizabethan architecture.

Clearly this treehouse was no impromptu structure – it was built to last. And if architecture is created with the intention of instilling a mood or a feeling, here is an example where those same magnificent qualities are applied to a tiny place of leisure.

soulful

Escapist, stylish and luxurious, the treehouses in this section are imbued with the spirit of romance, giving us the chance to dream and experience an alternative lifestyle. After spending some time reflecting and relaxing up high among the living branches and foliage, drifting back down to earth isn't that easy. These treehouses have been designed to create an immersive experience in a totally different atmosphere – as Andrew Marvell wrote, 'annihilating all that's made to a green thought in a green shade'.

Todd Oldham's design credentials are not restricted to product or fashion; his Pennsylvania treehouse retreat from New York city life is detailed, charming, whimsical and good-looking. The Brazilian treehouse of the Novogratz family wouldn't be out of place in a travel photo shoot with its timeless nod to colonial aesthetics and style. In the scented lavender fields of Lazio, north of Rome, we look at a twin treehouse holiday venue created by aesthetes and creative types, while a mere 20 minutes' drive from Florence is 'a treehouse with a view', the quintessence of romance. Often fuelled by a wish to create something calmer, an escape from career-driven city lives, these amazing structures are located in rural landscapes, making the expansive views as restful as their interiors.

It isn't just a visual thing, either; despite looking seriously stylish, several of these treehouse interiors underpin their good looks with equally respectful eco credentials. Are you ready to pull the cord pulley that raises a basket of locally produced organic honey, bread and fruit for breakfast to your treehouse? In many cases talented local craftsmen and furniture makers have been commissioned to furnish the interiors, using locally sourced materials in a site-specific way, which reflect the rusticity of the surrounding environment or take their inspiration from a nostalgia for the elegance of the past. The result in every case is a happy space which feels good to be in – warm and joyful.

amid the lavender fields

There are two treehouses on this beautiful Italian organic farm in the jaw-dropping countryside of northern Lazio between Tuscany and Rome, and both are the vision of Renzo Stucchi, a man whose career was forged in fashion but whose tastes remained unaffected by its fleeting trends and *haute couture* luxury. He yearned to escape city life to a rural retreat and moved his family here from Milan in 1999. The main building on the site, the eighteenth-century farmhouse, was in need of renovation, but Renzo was already looking beyond the hard graft and back through the vista of his years to a den that his father had built for him in an apricot tree when he was just eight years old. He had always hoped to recreate it and a chance meeting with a treehouse architect in Provence fuelled this desire.

Alain Laurens' designs were just what Renzo had been searching for and when he discovered a majestic centuries-old oak tree on his new property, his treehouse dream soon started to take shape. The treehouses, with their rustic yet chic interiors, were constructed in France and transported to Italy. Rising up out of a sea of 12 hectares (30 acres) of lavender fields, they stand alone and majestic. These charmed cabins are available to paying guests for a bed-and-breakfast style holiday as far removed from the hustle and bustle of everyday life as could be hoped for – when you're not elevated 7–8m (23–26ft) off the ground, you can linger in the olive groves, pick fresh vegetables and fruit and enjoy the homemade lavender honey and jam. In fact, the treehouses are so popular that you have to book them a year in advance.

style notes for suite bleue

It's a small, simple structure, yet the first time you see this treehouse it's hard not to draw comparisons of biblical proportions. Straddling the branches of a single spreading oak and commanding a view over the blue waves of lavender fields below, the treehouse readily brings to mind thoughts of Noah's Ark.

The tree on which Suite Bleue is built is purportedly one of the oldest in Italy. It's at least 600 years and stands 24m (78ft) high with a sturdy 4.5m (15ft) trunk. For Renzo, it was important that his building ambitions didn't affect the health of this heritage oak. The structure – an all-wooden pitch-roofed cabin, shed-like in its modesty – was dropped into the branches without a single nail to fix it in, and the tree continues to grow around its new houseguest. During thunderstorms an anti-impact electricity system creates a sort of cage that protects both the tree and cabin from potentially catastrophic bolts of lightning.

Renzo has arranged the furniture to create a shrine to symmetry. Identical tables flank each side of the bed, both with the same oil lantern. Two white cushions are arranged invitingly on the coverlet, while a pair of small bookshelves

mirrors each other on the upper corners of the wall. Sunlight pours in from the twin windows at the front gable end. The effect is one of harmony and balance.

In the external aesthetic, too, Renzo has shown enormous sensitivity. The structure isn't jarring in its environment; the lazy curve of the 8m (26ft) staircase seems the perfect extension of the rolling hills that surround it. Similarly, great care has been taken with the building materials. The treehouse is timber-clad inside and out, the rich tones complementing the supporting rough branches.

This rustic style informs the interior decor, albeit with a Provençal twist. Fabrics – all white – have a natural, homespun appeal. Far from being plain, the rich textures give understated elegance to the unassuming scheme. The reason for this restraint becomes obvious in June or July. Only then, when the lavender is in full bloom and a warm summer breeze billows the curtains, bringing the intoxicating scent indoors, do you realise this house isn't a cocoon from the outside world. Rather, it invites nature in to colour and perfume its every inch.

style notes for the black cabin

The first treehouse, Suite Bleue, proved enormously popular with guests, so much so that thought inevitably turned to the possibility of erecting a second treehouse on the site. This time a 200-year-old evergreen, a maritime pine, was the host tree, and 7m (23ft) above the ground is a simpler eco-loft treehouse, which is still ultra glamorous and luxe. Spacious and refined but also environmentally sustainable, it looks out over a beautiful pool, an olive grove and rolling hills, and from the deck there's even a sea view on clear days.

Built out of American red cedar, a wood that's naturally resistant to pests, the Black Cabin's materials and location may have intrinsic rustic qualities, but the style with which it is put together is something else. The interior, which is made from *bucchero* (a distinctive black Etruscan ceramic) as well as cedar, reinforces its upmarket credentials and demonstrates that guests won't be roughing it during their stay here. The space has a slick and sophisticated look with luxury fabrics yet simple furnishings that have been chosen thoughtfully with due attention to detail, from the organic bed linens to the lanterns. This is one of the largest treehouses in Europe at 87sq m (936sq ft) including the terrace.

Outside, off the deck a pulley system has been installed with a wooden box to send up essential supplies, along with your organic breakfast or even canapés and a glass of chilled white wine. The treehouse is simple, smart and very beautiful – Renzo and his wife Rosella have created a little slice of heaven among the lavender fields.

A sense of humour is evident in designer Todd Oldham's purpose-built two-storey treehouse in Pennsylvania. He instinctively understands what owning a treehouse is all about. 'Dangling 18m (60ft) up in the air, people instantly revert to being excited two-year-olds or cling to the railings in abject horror.' Todd looked at the classic literature of his childhood for inspiration and, with his partner Tony Longoria, set about creating a treehouse that would provide a stylish retreat.

It's often a good idea to add some childhood nostalgia and rustic charm to the mix, even if the end result has modern leanings. He pooled his ideas, consulting with companies that create playgrounds and adventure wilderness experiences, to make the project a reality. Consequently, the treehouse feels playful and fun but also real and honest – a place to exist and be happy.

The structure, externally and internally clad with wood, is accessed via an angled stairway. It has a handmade feel: the exterior surfaces and deck are created from rougher, textural feather-edged wood while the interior has a smoother, more finished and decorative treatment. Narrow birch wood trunks and branches have been crafted into open mezzanine sleeping platforms and ladders, which are etched with drawings, notations and doodles – references to idle afternoons and romantic wanderings – like the top of many school desks, notebooks or pieces of bark. Similarly, but of a more sophisticated ethos, the backs of shelves are set in a classic herringbone marquetry, and the walls and floor in varying toned, vertical strip wooden panels.

A wood-clad TV, desk and upholstered seating area means that being able to live here is also a practical experience. Todd's plan to create an ambience with a touch of humour in the design has been successful. 'I don't feel like a kid when I'm up here, but I do feel like a really happy adult.'

todd oldham's treehouse

style notes

This clever creation combines freedom and adventure. It's a confident and happy space – a sheer delight in form and colour. It's powerful combinations such as this that make a space feel good, and although it's fun, uncompromising quality is evident throughout.

Todd Oldham knows exactly what a treehouse retreat should represent – there's nothing stark, dank or gloomy here. On the contrary, it's warm, functional and joyful. Each object is coveted, enjoyed, considered and a niche has been found for it. Like the details of an imaginatively crafted film set, every piece is a distillation of many things, chosen and designed for what it means and signifies for the owner and helping create a beautiful and eclectic backdrop. Every graphic note has been squeezed out of the wood within, its tones and textures playfully juxtaposed and celebrated. No detail has been overlooked nor any opportunity missed; even the backs of the chairs have a wooden pattern spiral laid in the wood.

The delight in form is everywhere: small woodland creatures nestle comfortably alongside a vibrant collection of vases and paintings of dogs and cats. Although there's a plethora of wooden textures, shapes and forms, this is not an overly cluttered or overwhelming space. Colours and brushmarks punch through in the textiles, paintings and objects. Bland mass production has been stamped out in favour of the individual one-off find: quirky pieces are sprinkled about and the space is all about individuality, a celebration of design and low and high art. Todd has relished the details and you sense that each time you visit this space, you could unearth more; even the exterior windowsills have a gentle wash of leaf green.

brazilian beachfront treehouse

In Trancosco, a former fishing village on Brazil's Bahia coast, is a treehouse that represents the best of the town's sleepy, laid-back and stylish aesthetic. From its humble origins, the town became popular in the 1970s with an influx of bohemian Sao Paolo folk in the same way that many northern Europeans were attracted to Ibiza or Marrakech. All these people were seeking artful, relatively undiscovered places of languid beauty that were off the beaten track.

A designer friend mentioned the 'cool' coastal town to Robert and Courtney Novogratz of Sixx Design. Creative, entrepreneurial and travel-loving, they started exploring the legalities of property ownership for foreign nationals and, finding it was possible, their treehouse project became a reality. They use it as their holiday home but rent it out at other times.

As a couple they have a formidable design pedigree and are very experienced at buying and converting inspiring properties, but in this case they took a different approach. Using talented local furniture makers and craftspeople, Robert and Courtney were able not only to create something really individual and site-specific but also to commission the exact furniture they required – a simple sketch on a napkin was all it took.

The preference for local materials favours wood, so this enterprising couple used it, together with other natural materials and finishes as well as happy colours, when they set about creating an extraordinary space. In the process they referenced direct influences from their surroundings – even the showers are cleverly crafted from tree trunks.

style notes

This treehouse was created by a couple with a genuine interest in form and colour. Hence they find beauty in the simplest objects and furniture: clothes are hung from a plain bar while decorative bespoke vases, simple woven mats and lampshades comfortably define the space. There are framed textiles, a vintage freestanding mirror and a painted surfboard leaning casually against a wall.

Similarly, their love of design, craft skills and detail inform the interior. Inside this classy yet rustic and naturalistic holiday home, every corner has been carefully considered, and it is filled with uncontrived, understated luxury. A palette of wood tones, with notes of cream and white and hints of turquoise blue weave through the treehouse, along with rich accents of texture and colour.

There are also touches and references of timeless and elegant colonial beauty, including a central ceiling fan, the four-poster bed with its diaphanous muslin drapes and a very modern round washbasin supported by a traditional wooden washstand with highly crafted and carefully turned legs and a shelf underneath for wicker baskets of towels and toiletries.

The external environment, too, is reflected in the stylish interior: the light switches are housed in wooden boxes, and the showers are fashioned from tree trunks, their heads emerging from ingeniously hollowed-out branches, while the pebble-surfaced walls and flooring root you as clearly as can be in this sophisticated yet understated arboreal home.

tuscan treehouse

Think of Florence and you conjure up E.M. Forster's classic novel *A Room with a View* – the romance, rolling hills and Renaissance architecture. And Casa Barthel, just 20 minutes from Florence's dreamy cityscape, has that 'view'. In the book, Mr Emerson asserts that there is only one perfect view – the sky above us. Well, this treehouse has that too, thanks to a beguiling little skylight in the bedroom ceiling. The dark wood surround of the cut-out serves to frame the clouds that occasionally scud overhead, effectively creating a moving picture.

This nod to the art world is no accident. Casa Barthel is the work of design aficionada and architect Elena Barthel. Her treehouse is part of a hilltop hamlet of characterful cottages, olive groves and vines, which are open to paying guests. Elena shares the space with her husband Andrew as well as her mother, brother and his wife, aunt and uncle and her 90-year-old grandmother. As well as sharing a love of the countryside, they also have some creative genes in common. The Barthels have a design studio in the city and the family are renowned for their hand-painted tiles and for commissioning artisans to breathe new life into antique furniture. A small army of carpenters, upholsterers and bronzers work tirelessly for them to salvage Italian treasures, restoring or creatively adapting pieces for a new purpose.

Elena seems to have inherited this knack for revision. For her the handsome pine trees dotting the land don't just provide welcome shade from the blazing Tuscan sun – they are also the stilts for a leafy new treehouse home in the canopy – a cleverly designed refuge of wood, glass and steel with a panorama to die for.

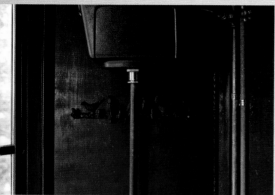

style notes

For what is a relatively small space, this charming treehouse accommodates modern domestic conveniences adeptly. As well as a queen-sized bed, decorative wood burner, air conditioning, kitchenette and terrace, Elena has also found room for an oversized rain shower and separate lavatory tucked away behind the bedroom. The chalkboard walls sum up the Barthel family's collaborative nature rather well – they invite our active participation. Guests aren't just engaging with the natural world by sleeping among the stars; they're also reaching out to each other and the guests before and after them by leaving witty messages and pictures. This sense of community and family is intrinsically Italian and is evident outside in the mini-piazza directly underneath the treehouse – perfect for long convivial meals with loved ones.

Elena describes the arboreal loft as a 'romantic' space. From the russet red and coppery hues that warm the rooms to the periodic lick of decadence (like the fur throw covering the bed), these luxurious notes quietly challenge the otherwise minimalist and lightly industrial feel. With so many exposed metal beams and copper pipework both inside and outside, these softer touches are important. They make the metalwork feel more like an enveloping nest rather than an enclosing cage.

And still there's room for the odd twinge of nostalgia. Maybe it's Forster's influence again, but it's hard not to feel a turn-of-the-century vibe in the station luggage rack that serves as shelves in the kitchen, the richly polished wood of the ceiling and picture frames or even the green accents of the terrace furniture. It's updated Edwardian style with an Italian twist – and it's a breath of fresh air.

handmade

When talent and time are given generously, the human hand is capable of incredible work, whether it's conceptual or practical, and in this chapter we focus on the nature of that handiwork and its intention in the creation of some extraordinary treehouses that are the stuff of dreams. All highly individualistic, they combine a high-spec finish and quality with superb craftsmanship.

On Dartmoor, a sinuous, beautifully curving cocoon of a treehouse pod stops you dead in your tracks, and although it's handcrafted, it's about as far from a rickety, ramshackle treehouse as you can imagine. Inspired by the nest of the weaver bird, it's extraordinary in its originality and structural form. On the other side of the Atlantic in Brooklyn, New York City, frustrated by the post-graduation creative opportunities available to her, Alexandra Meyn created her own brief and designed and built a treehouse, which is the essence of funkiness, with discarded and recycled materials in the backyard of her rental apartment.

And, finally, there's the lucky couple who were the recipients of the stunning Sauna Treehouse, a highly unusual wedding present. Its design and conception relate as much to legend and myth as they do to the trees themselves. Restorative and beautiful, it looms over the landscape in its visionary grandeur. These are quirky treehouses that are sublimely inventive and whose creation is both individual and inspired.

brooklyn backyard treehouse

Backyard treehouses are the stuff of dreams, especially in overcrowded cities, and definitely not just for young families. Alexandra Meyn had just finished her master's degree in Interior design and was looking for a project she could get her teeth into and use as an expression of her aesthetic. With a tiny $400 budget, she determined upon the idea of a treehouse.

The backyard of her rented ground-floor Bedford-Stuyvesant New York apartment was no lush urban park: it was a paved area with a 12m (40ft) mulberry tree incongruously growing in it. With the permission of her landlord and the help of 12 friends, the construction of a 4.5sq m (48sq ft) and 5m (17ft) tall treehouse took shape. The tree was not used as a support but rather as a fixed focal point with the structure conceived on a platform around its girth. Alexandra used found and repurposed materials, including cedar shingles, old glazed French doors and items sourced from community projects selling reclaimed building materials. She carefully kept the build size within the permitted development parameters of a recreation space.

She wanted to use the the treehouse as a hang-out, a summer night sleep-out and a painting studio. Practical and straightforward, she ran a cable from her bedroom to power a string of lights and a record player. By gathering as many ideas as possible, the structure took shape. Unsurprisingly, it is beyond the ordinary – a tin roof, sash-paned windows hung individually to float freely like a giant mobile, and French doors opening outwards rather than inwards create a glass house. Alexandra understands the potency of the treehouse as a concept: 'I think everyone has this special place in their brain, a primal nostalgia, for a treehouse'.

style notes

The treehouse was described by Jason Holmes, a friend who worked with Alexandra on the construction, as 'southern funkiness'. As he says: 'There's an aesthetic in New Orleans that's rustic and funky and weathered in a way that you only see in a warmer climate. It's evident in Alexandra's work and in this treehouse.' There is a confidence here that's embodied by the mixture of materials and finishes and the way they've been put together, which creates the style and ambience of a French atelier's workshop – high up, luminous, light and airy. Brilliantly opposed to the dark and slightly gloomy wooden treehouses of our childhood, this unique space feels expanded and engaging.

The design is recycled but coherent: there is a strong aesthetic that plays on colour and light and an obvious love of materials and textures. Alexandra takes inspiration from her New Orleans' roots and her tastes are eclectic but considered – funky and layered. The patchwork of colour and textures knitted together has created a space with a delightful patina of weathered wood, recycled paper, peeling paint and rusting tin.

With its memories, musical cadences and weathered, chipped and resilient finishes, it evokes the soulful qualities that Alexandra is striving to find. Determined and resourceful, she has a passion for collecting and honing in on the overlooked, and she has created a scrapbook of a space, using interesting design elements and finding beauty in the discarded or recycled. Although it's a humble structure, it's a very accomplished piece of design.

It took only five days to create this striking treehouse, which was inspired by a weaver bird's nest and constructed as part of a 'spatial structures' course during Dartmoor Arts Week in Devon, England. The brief from the local landowners and farmers was to produce a safe play space for their grandchildren. Working collaboratively with students and the carpenter Henry Russell, Jerry Tate Architects identified a suitable structurally sound mature oak tree on a steep hill as the ideal site. It provided an open and far-reaching aspect over the surrounding countryside and other builds from previous years' competitions.

This unique treehouse takes the form of a pod 1.8m (6ft) in diameter and with a circular seat within its 10sq m (107sq ft). Access is via a walkway that climbs up the steep slope to the tree. The structural form and physical qualities of the weaver bird's nest appealed to Tate because it looks 'dramatic but safe and secure'.

Using locally felled and milled timber – spruce, larch and western red cedar – the structure took shape. It was attached to the tree by means of two fixings. Thin lathes of spruce, some laminated together to form 'ribs', were used to provide structural form while other lathes were woven together to create different densities of covering as well as strength.

dartmoor cocoon treehouse

style notes

Simple and sensitive, from every conceivable angle, this is a handmade structure that delights us – the overlapping spruce ribs beautifully bind the treehouse. It is tactile and reminiscent of a three-dimensional manifestation of a geometric string drawing. Stitched together precisely, it has a dynamic feel as if it belongs to the natural world and wasn't created by humans. Within this considered design, the organic nature of the structure has been curbed and controlled.

As with most weaver birds' nests, it has a narrow entrance facing downwards, and a flask-shaped chamber at the top. The wide flat lathes are irregularly spaced, each playing its part in creating the space as a whole. The wooden walkway functions as a transition zone. Starting on a higher piece of land, with the entranceway relatively tall and open, its height decreases as you near the nest/pod, which is contained and secure.

This simple yet elegant form is as much a piece of sculpture as a treehouse and safe play space for children. But if treehouses are all about taking you to another place, another reality, touching nature more closely and having an adventure, here is a beautiful example of this concept in action. As the architect Jerry Tate said: 'Nature is a sublime designer'.

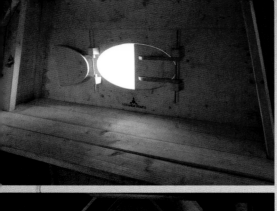

sauna treehouse

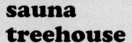

This unique free-standing wooden structure, which resembles a giant bird, is actually a very unusual outdoor sauna that was designed to create a thoughtful and reflective space. Sited in a valley near Piacenza in Italy, it was commissioned as a very special wedding present. It's the creation of the Milan-based architecture studio AtelierFORTE, whose founder Duilio Forte says: 'The sauna is positioned so that people can enter an intimate environment that nurtures conversation and interaction'. This design follows the principles of The New Sublimity – the growing trend for people who feel alienated by consumerism and globalisation to escape from their busy digital lifestyles and seek a new more contemplative identity, values and authenticity. The treehouse is called 'Huginn and Muninn' after the two ravens of the Norse god Odin. Every day he sent them out flying across the earth and they came back and told him everything they had seen and heard. There is an analogy with the sauna – a moment of reflection and relaxation at the end of a long day.

The interior and exterior are both made in spruce, described by Duilio as 'a very simple wood that doesn't need much insulation but which is powerful and strong'. The heat for the sauna is generated by a woodburning stove. The exterior openings are small, oval shuttered windows through which you can view the wide panorama of the northern Italian landscape. Rather than close-up details, what you see from this high vantage point must be similar to that of a bird flying overhead. With its fixed gigantic beaklike projections, this structure references the natural world and is intended as a spiritual space as well as a physical one.

style notes

Drawing its inspiration from the raven messengers of Norse legend, this innovative structure really does seem to be poised to move and take flight. The roof tips are angular whereas the interior has been kept deliberately simple, restorative and restful. The exterior finish is painted a dark matt grey in parts – a colour inspired by the hues of the crow – while the remaining areas have the natural finish of its spruce construction.

The internal space is reached via a simple wooden ladder, creating a metaphorical journey upwards, and up there, off the ground, away from the everyday, a physical and mental transition occurs. This is a restful space where the connection between the recollection and the retelling of the day's journey can hopefully take place.

This quirky treehouse is designed to be easy on the eye as well as the soul – a respite and a cathartic space just a flight away from the 'full on' nature of modern life. Poetic and charming, it seems with its strong silhouette to be perched on the roof of the world, cutting a strong cinematic form against the softer undulating Italian landscape and the vast expanse of sky. It could easily have come from the fantastical inventive sketchbook of a film production designer.

But it's real, not fantasy, and it is a practical space where people can chill, rest, talk and take stock before re-emerging, refreshed and invigorated. There's no doubt that the design, however stunning, is idiosyncratic, but beneath its exterior drama and the spruce lies a conceptually coherent piece of art, inspiring and rejuvenating. What a gift!

art installations

Art can often take itself mighty seriously and, although they are not trivial, these installations are the real cutting edge – forward and sideways looking, utterly fearless. The ideas behind them are extraordinary but, once seen, these spaces and their vision distil down into our more regular lives. They inspire an empowering feeling of possibility and a courageousness, which are both to be welcomed. Art is most powerful when it fires your imagination and takes you on an escapist journey out of your habitual everyday life to new and unfamiliar territory, as evidenced by the treehouses in this section.

The New York Gallery Treehouse is an artwork in itself as well as a unique arboreal environment for displaying art in a wide range of media. This non-traditional space parts company with convention and forces you to look at artworks in a new way, to connect with the natural world around you and even question the nature of art itself. It is enriching, humbling and human.

The Artist's Fruitcase Treehouse, set up in a tree high on top of a tower block, creates an unexpected sight in the urban centre of Amsterdam but hints at a variety of themes, including necessity, isolation, recycling and resourceful creation. And, never far from our love of caravans and a life on the road, the subversive Caravan in the Sky is a humorous, relevant and inspiring installation. It speaks of respite and adventure – and it's pretty cool-looking, too. In both these installations, familiar and conventional forms and materials have been used to create something arresting and visually striking.

artist's fruitcrate treehouse

At first glance it is easy to see that this is a treehouse made of recycled fruit and vegetable crates. And as well as being an attractive structure, it's an inspirational, affordable and creative concept. Its startling location inevitably raises some questions – it's 50m (164ft) off the ground in a tree supported by guy ropes that seems to be growing out of the top of a modern building in the centre of Amsterdam – but, in reality, this is a site-specific art installation, which was created in 2004 as part of an exhibition at the Stedelijk Museum, devoted to modern and contemporary art and design. It was designed by the Dutch contemporary artist Leonard van Munster, who believes that art has to be experienced rather than just viewed.

Van Munster built the treehouse off-site and he would climb into it at night, a light shining from the building when it was occupied. Its construction appears haphazard, traditionally shaped but ramshackle – the strips of coloured graphic-printed wood are not set neatly. This is a personal rather than a professional build, as if speed and freedom were of the essence, and it was constructed intuitively without much planning. The branches that grow out of the 10m (33ft) high tree support the rudimentary structure that just about fulfils its purpose. Its design and incongruous location are an experience for the viewer as well as the occupant.

Beyond the obvious sense and value of reusing attractive everyday materials, especially those with visual character, this simple building represents what a small separate space can offer us. Its exaggerated, extreme location makes the point clearly: it's a shelter, a thing of beauty and a refuge in what can sometimes be an uncomfortable world.

style notes

Art works best when it informs, fires your imagination and transports you on a temporary magical journey of possibility. View this witty, imaginative and beautiful installation and, for a moment, you will experience the sense that the parameters of space and their world have been redefined. The structure has a tactile quality, with its familiar patchwork of the printed sides of lightweight wooden but protective fruit boxes, each with its own story of a long journey from sunnier climes...originating, no doubt, far away as protective and transportable packaging. However, instead of being discarded, these graphic materials have been reused to create a new, albeit temporary, home for someone.

This incredible skyline installation resonates with all of us. It's almost magical – a tree perched on a tall building with a small, fragile but tangible and real space balancing on top. It looks so frail that you feel it could disappear in the blink of an eye and with a strong gust of wind. As a piece of art, it's testimony to the fact that when art is elevated from the more formal sphere of a gallery, there are limitless possibilities for the viewer as well as the artist.

As the inspiration for a real treehouse, Under heaven 01, as it is known, takes some beating. The material construction and simple form are visually attractive and eminently affordable. On a human level, it connects with our valuable and rich communal experience of escapism, solitude and separation as well as fun, and focuses attention on the intrinsic value that a simple treehouse can give to its creator, occupants and spectators.

caravan in the sky

When you first glimpse French artist Benedetto Bufalino's work, you are reminded that humour and art can be brilliantly and, seemingly, effortlessly intertwined. Located in streets, parks and gardens, his creations are intentionally temporary and instantly recognisable forms. His art is witty, subversive and all about communicating on a human level. This installation in a French town is a nod to the spirit of a treehouse – the Skyjack lift of an angular vintage caravan. There is the suggestion of people clustered within thanks to the partially drawn curtains.

As with all treehouses, it has escaped the bounds of earth and, in so doing, it attempts to create its own imaginary alternative world. The everyday and mediocre have been delightfully tweaked into something that is both visually striking and beautiful, transforming the humble caravan into a powerful and awe-inspiring image. The parameters of space and logic have been redefined and the viewer is integral to this escapist adventure.

style notes

Benedetto's approach was to use simple materials, and he fashioned this installation out of wood in the simple squared-off form of a 1960s family caravan. He created an inner structural piece that could be fixed to a hired scissor lift and then added the outer wooden skin. A structural engineer checked its stability and safety before the caravan was raised 14m (46ft) up into the air. Connected to mains electricity, the caravan lights glow at night.

The angles of the caravan seem to complement the zigzag jack: it's as if it was predestined to be elevated above the earth. The blue line, an unremarkable design detail, is given a new boldness and significance when it appears on a caravan that has been pinned to the sky.

This site-specific installation was designed to be temporary, but it proved so popular that it's still there, hovering above the town. Benedetto's intention was 'to invent a futuristic caravan that was its own kind of utopia' and that's exactly what he has created.

gallery treehouse

As with many things in life, good ideas sometimes happen as the result of the seed of an idea combining with an unexpected opportunity. For artist Amanda Wong and her partner Andrew Shirley, the concept of creating a treehouse gallery space came about when a friend asked them to manage his country property in New York State. Together with an area of woodland with stately sugar maple trees, the barns and outbuildings contained 'a hundred years of junk and detritus', so they had the space, the location and the materials to build a treehouse.

By identifying with nature, Amanda wanted to 'create a non-traditional space to house or showcase works of art'. The 'gallery' experience was all about integrating the audience into the space to genuinely engage with art rather than viewing it clinically. The design for the largely open treehouse took an unconventional route and the project developed in an 'anti-architectural' based process. However, Amanda stayed faithful to her key concepts: the large, wall-sized windows that keep the interior well lit, and, as a gesture towards openness, the 'no doors' rule. Her plan was to use only appropriate or recycled materials within a strict budget.

Up in the tree, however, there were no restrictions and the message of the surrounding organic shapes and contours was clearly that they needed to be flexible. By not using direct ground supports other than the tree – well, three trees to be precise – they harnessed an organic combination of different growth rates and movements. The whole process was enlightening – nature takes over and adapts constantly, and the trees embody this idea.

style notes

Using only scavenged locally sourced materials gives you the opportunity to let happenstance provide a range of randomly achieved visual finishes. An old lake pier yielded white wooden planks, which were used on the walls facing the river; the southern exterior walls came from a red painted barn door. There was some creative tinkering, too. The couple considered painting the treehouse black to make it virtually invisible at night. They were fascinated by burned-out buildings and a Japanese wood treatment called Shou-Sugi-Ban, which waterproofs and repels bugs by means of scorching the wood. Amanda discovered the simplest way to achieve this effect was to run the wooden boards through the flames of a bonfire to char them.

The treehouse and its environment provide a flexible living backdrop to the art shows, such as one by the artist Andrew Poneros with his sand-blasted glass chandeliers. He installed a large

chandelier from the ceiling using 2 x 4 wood, while in the trees along the riverbank he built shelves on which he balanced illuminated vases. His works, composed of glass and themed with light and water, beautifully complemented the treehouse and its river setting.

This is a treehouse with an unconventional purpose, design process, material sourcing, funding and construction. Its roots lie in Amanda's artistry and Andrew's childhood memories. Now it's art and fun that go on inside and outside their treehouse, together with an openness to share the experience. The etched names of an unknown romantic couple are scratched into a heart on the side of this hospitable place that welcomes everyone.

eclectic

Doing your own thing, collecting ideas from different sources – from experience, imagination and a mixture of references and influences – is enriching, and being able to peek into the minds and creations of people that have already done so is always a joy. The results are rich, exciting, meaningful and deeply satisfying; each element and influence brings its own value and characteristics to the mix. The results are always creative and they make you stop and look.

London couple Karen Luchtenstein and Willie Smax have creative CVs to die for as well as a garden treehouse and bar area that similarly inspire. Using largely found materials, they have woven a rich mixture of materials, objects and design into an entire lifestyle for their friends and family. You'd want to spend time there, hanging out, lounging, chatting and happily idling. In another backyard but this time in Utah, leather worker and motorcycle enthusiast Quinn Petersen has used his design genius to upcycle some discarded materials and transform them into a cosy and unusual treehouse.

Meanwhile, in Tennessee, with her frugal modernist approach, Collyn at ModFruGal has found an expression for her twist on modernist design within a budget. In a totally different environment on the beautiful Cornish coast of southwest England, Sparrow House feels as if Jack Sparrow might just turn up any minute with his booty. It is wild and remote: the wind blew relentlessly throughout our photo shoot, but magically transformed when a double rainbow emerged from the storm...see what I mean?

frugal modernism

This modernist take on a treehouse distills the key elements down to simple elegant forms. It's the brainchild of the resourceful and talented owner of ModFruGal. She has designed something that has all the hallmarks of perfection but on a remarkably small budget. The structure, size and proportions were determined by the stock sizes of the available materials in the local timber yard. This 'treehouse' is not supported by a tree and, technically, is not a real treehouse at all but rather a house up amongst the trees.

The owner's approach to its construction was pragmatic, realistic and economical in terms of labour, time and waste. Up in the tree, the platform and a sturdy wooden access ladder were constructed first. Each side panel was built and stained separately at accessible ground level and then hauled up on the horizontal, one by one, onto the platform before being raised by 90 degrees to the vertical, 'barn style'. The roof was constructed with a layer of tar paper between the plywood base and corrugated metal finishing. Polycarbonate sheets were used as skylights.

The interior floor space measures a small 2.4 x 2.4m (8 x 8ft), set onto a 2.4 x 3.7m (8 x 12ft) platform under a roof covering. The dimensions were chosen to minimize waste, using standard, big-box lumber lengths. The family acknowledges that they would have liked it to be bigger but it would have changed the approach and increased the budget.

style notes

A confident and unpretentious space, this is welcoming and practical with a rich use of materials, colours and textures. It could be conceived as a den or hideaway. The horizontal structural timbers are used as shelving, and the owner's aversion to natural toned plywood is dealt with by adding a swift daub of taupe. The interior floors have two layers of woodstain and a finishing coat of varnish. Space is wonderfully maximized: the daybed is composed of two twin air mattresses stacked on top of each other. All you need do is move the coffee table (which holds the two hammocks) and lay the mattresses on the floor. The windows have sliding acrylic covers to retain the heat inside in winter and keep the pollen out during the spring.

And the exterior is no less impressive, cutting a beautiful silhouette among the trees of the forest. The sharp red chairs on the decking are as bold and striking as a scarlet wax seal on an envelope. At the front is a sliding barn door; painted a dark brown, it sits well within the woodland. Access is by wooden ladder steps, with a length of plumbing pipe as a handrail.

The key to the success of this treehouse is the owner's vision. Her bold and confident use of colour is simple, uncomplicated and powerful. And rather than reproduce modernist mid-century design and styling she has reinterpreted it, moved it on and created a delightfully modern hybrid – frugal modernism has found its expression.

london chill-out treehouse

Treehouses often start off as family projects created specially for children. Here's an example of one that has changed over time, graduating into an urban oasis that has grown up to be a very cool piece of heaven for all the family. Painter Karen Lutchenstein and her husband Willie Smax are one of those super-talented creative couples. A big consideration for them when they were househunting in London was finding a sizeable back garden that wasn't overlooked and which felt as though they had been transported to the country.

They set about building their young sons a treehouse, using mostly reclaimed timber that was scavenged or found on skips. Inspired by Willie's vision, it began life as a platform with a flying fox rope and a fireman's pole, but the boys liked it so much that he doubled its size and began to build a house, working around the tree from the floor up, with Karen as his 'assistant'.

Under the vertical stilt supports they created a seating area, and as time passed and the boys hit their teens, they saw the potential for transforming this area. Adding a brick floor and using reclaimed timber enabled an outdoor bar and kitchen to take shape. Karen painted it a soft green with rust details to enliven it and dug a trench to bring hot and cold water from her garden studio. It became a purposeful space with a 1940s cooker fuelled by a gas bottle, making it easy to brew a cup of tea or even make jam from the fruit trees in the garden – or other cooking tasks that might stink out the kitchen in the house. But let's not forget this is a bar and the natural inclination is to have a party! The treehouse now has a more grown-up role; as part of the bar area, it functions as an upstairs chill-out and quiet conversation area.

style notes

Making full use of the luxury of their large outdoor space, Karen and Willie tapped into the homestead aesthetic in the design and build of the treehouse and bar. Architecturally this is a simple classic structure, as if you were sketching a rudimentary ideal tiny house, with a wavy gabled end, a small balustraded verandha and horizontally clad walls. Inside it's calm and serene. There's a daybed where you can sit, lounge or snooze with large squashy cushions. Narrow shelves house books and art materials – quiet encouragements to engage a creative mind. Will has made a built-in bench using feet from a broken armchair and fitted with an old mattress and cushions covered in discontinued Indian fabric. The striped curtains are sewn from some old deckchair covers. The windows are varied, with obscured textured glass and leaded light designs, and the soft light inspires contemplation. The rear walls use the same leaded glass, bought at a car boot sale, but placed high up as skylights.

Downstairs, beneath the corrugated overhang roof, the focus is on creating a friendly communality. There are high bar stools, found at the bargain corner in IKEA, painted in different colours to use up cans of paint from other jobs around the house. Collected materials and vintage items have found a new purpose here. A classic popcorn maker, teapot, vintage crockery, decorative old tins and storage canisters are not only functional but look gorgeous. They set the scene and make you want to linger, hang out, chat and join in.

sparrow house

In freakishly wild and windy weather, the Sparrow House on the Lizard Peninsula in Cornwall creaks and sways, clinging onto an ash tree and connecting you to the visceral and elemental experience of living within the natural world. It's the brainchild of Jonathan Melville-Smith, who wanted to develop some unusual holiday accommodation.

He embarked on an organic, fluid build that was barely designed at all and came from a more physical but no less cerebral process, working on site, tools in hand. Locating a suitably sturdy tree, he built a platform with a protection rail. From there, strips of wood were attached to the platform, wrapped over the rail and joined at the top. With his understanding of how wood bends and his experience in joinery and carpentry, Jonathan just let things happen, and the shape and structure of the treehouse emerged, from only available materials. Harnessing his natural inability to throw things away, he had most of what he needed from his own house-building and conversion projects, and only the remaining 20 per cent were scavenged.

The house was simple: sited 2m (6ft 6in) off the ground, it had one 2.4m (8ft) square main living area with seating and a small kitchen while a mezzanine level provided a double bedroom. Access is by a wooden staircase, the interior is insulated, and the windows are double glazed. Nearby there's a toilet and separate shower at ground level. This is a comfortable space, supplied with electricity via a camping-style hook-up and mains water. It is heated in winter and there's a cool box for food storage, a two-burner hob and grill, and a washbasin – all the essentials of life distilled down to the minimum.

style notes

The exterior is architecturally robust with huge windows cutting a clean and majestic line through the façade and out over the landscape. The idiosyncratic shape takes a nod in the direction of the green canvas-roofed gypsy roulettes but rises to a curved pointed apex, like a vertical leaf. You ascend via a ladder with branches woven around it. It feels romantic and magical, transporting you into an ivy-clad other world of adventure and escape. According to Jonathan, 'The tree grew into it and it grew with the tree and became part of the tree'.

The barrel-like interior is warm and cosy, a taste of life on the open road, connecting with the countryside while providing refuge from the elements. Offering a hint of folkloric myth, more tree branches are used inside, sparingly on the edged shelves, while found objects are utilised as hooks. This is not contrived, hard-worn or spartan but comfortable and well equipped for self-sufficiency – from the jars of coffee to the whistling kettle. Historic and timeless, the wood-clad interior is a masterclass in how to create a pared-down feel without losing life's essential comforts. The bed is suspended in the rafters, submerged in a cocoon-like, draped muslin-tented ceiling with muffled soft fairy lights and textural quilts.

Style-wise, this treehouse has a delicacy and sensitivity; it's imaginative and enveloping. Elevated and removed from the world, you feel unreachable. The creaking branches and the hooting of owls are the real-life sound effects – the genuine treehouse experience.

utah leather worker's treehouse

Quinn Petersen is the first to admit his backyard treehouse bucks the trend. For a start, rather than being suspended sky high in the leafy canopy, it sits close to the ground. It wasn't supposed to be a treehouse at all – he ran out of space in his garage and wanted a platform cover for his motorbikes. He modestly claims that the deck and roof just evolved. Owning a treehouse had always appealed to him, but he had no mature trees. His brainwave – to suspend it between a cluster of Chinese elms next to his driveway – came late one night while he was tossing and turning in bed, and he began constructing it the very next day.

The biggest challenge was working with five separate trees: 'During a storm, they naturally want to move and tear the treehouse apart'. To prevent this tension on the structure it was built low to the ground (there is less movement towards the base of the tree, enabling a more stable building) and the floor was pinned by seven bolts. He built a rubber skirt to allow some movement in the same way as a ship at sea when it's anchored but still able to oscillate.

Quinn describes the trees as 'trashy', but if anyone knows how to turn unloved pieces into design genius it's him. He owns a company that makes artisan wallets, bags and ties, mainly from reclaimed vintage fabrics. Upcycling is the theme of his treehouse, too, including the standout feature wall of repurposed windows. He already had a few left over from previous projects, while the rest were collected from antique stores and yard sales. All the wood is recycled from the old fascia on his house, which was used to repair rain gutters. The gorgeous wooden chair was rehomed after it was discarded in a neighbourhood rubbish bin.

style notes

The large patchwork of windows, with their Mondrian-like criss-cross of lines, dominates the interior. Quinn has cleverly chosen pieces that work with this feature rather than trying to compete with it. The glass chandelier is a case in point. Seemingly incongruous amid the laid-back furnishings and unfinished walls, it is also easily assimilated, refracting the light and echoing the glass of the windows. This sensitivity is on display elsewhere, too. Quinn is adept at stitching together difficult materials. In this creation, the trees surrounding the house act like huge needles piercing and weaving through the skin of the wood.

He's also got a keen eye for texture, marrying the warm, weathered patina of the tongue-and-groove panelling to the glint of tin on the roof and the sculpted metal of his motorbikes, standing like sentries on guard duty below. They make you feel that the cabin is not just a retreat but a small fortress defending Quinn's commitment to the handcrafted, creative spirit of America that is threatened by today's mass consumerism. A 'drawbridge' ladder up to the treehouse tucks neatly away when not in use, providing a visible and real disconnect from the world outside. Rather modestly, Quinn concedes that this is a 'pretty neat addition'. While he was leading a workshop with a local scout group, they clambered in, drew up the ladder and pretended they were in a spaceship. This treehouse proves that stretching your architectural imagination will take you anywhere you want to go.

businesses

Without doubt, treehouses create a mood and atmosphere. They are, by nature, special – a world away from the ordinary. To capitalise on this is smart, and the businesses that we feature here achieve this in differing ways: some out of necessity, as is the case with the game reserves of Africa; others, such as the Welsh Living Room, by inviting people to engage and immerse more fully in a sustainable natural world. And some, like the treehouse restaurants, create a destination in themselves, a memorable landmark.

These treehouses have required courage, not only in their execution but also in satisfying local building and safety regulations that govern their suitability for opening to the public. In the giant trees in the grounds of Alnwick Castle in Northumberland is a delightful treehouse restaurant complex, which was commissioned and designed to be magical and foster fairy-tale imaginings. On a humbler scale, the restaurant in the cool district of East Nashville is more themic. The treehouse, its defining feature, is emblematic of the transformation of what was once the musician Buddy Spicher's bungalow into a hip hang-out.

Meanwhile in deepest Wales the Living Room treehouses are an ecologically sound holiday accommodation business without losing their innate sense of style and design in the pursuit of sustainability. And on this worldwide treehouse journey we couldn't resist the safari treetops of Africa. High up above the veldt, these provide a real wilderness experience. We look at both the glamorous and the more down-to-earth in style, but although they are all gorgeous none of them can truly compete with the real wildlife action just below your feet.

safari treehouses

As sleep-outs go, an exposed platform in the African bush is quite extreme. This may be part of a luxurious, high-end resort, but when the sun goes down and the wide, black night comes alive to the sounds of growls, grunts, hums, cackles, buzzes and roars, it's hard not to dwell on the fact that you're a part of nature and sharing the space with some extraordinary neighbours. The open air treehouses offer safety, luxury, and a fabulous vantage point on the fringe of one of the largest game reserves on the continent.

Lion Sands is a South African safari complex with history. Its treehouses are an intrinsic part of a holiday experience comprising lodges with private pools and opulent interiors. They are sited on a family-owned property that dates back four generations to a Virginian gold miner turned stockbroker who arrived in 1933 to hunt big game before turning conservationist. Legend has it that the founder Guy Aubrey Chalkley set up camp in a native leadwood tree, having been chased up it by predators roaming the dusty veldt below.

These are treehouses that repay patient scrutiny. They are the ultimate bush bedrooms with five-star creature comforts as well as spectacular views. You could easily spend hours quietly surveying the wildlife around you: the timid, graceful springbok and skulking packs of hyenas. Here, Africa doesn't just open up at a distance below, you're part of it.

style notes for the chalkley treehouse

Approaching the Chalkley treehouse, you could be mistaken for thinking you are in the middle of a Brothers Grimm fairy tale, so extraordinarily unsettling is the silhouette of the tree supporting it. The tree is bone dry and with gnarled fingers stretching upwards to the sky. There's something hunched and witch-like about the shadows it throws over the platform. Its common name, leadwood, perfectly describes just how dense and resilient these trees are. They can remain standing, bare and skeletal like this one, for up to 80 years after dying.

Located 4.5km (2.7 miles) from the main lodge, the treehouse rests 9m (30ft) above the ground and is principally a simple open platform. Access is via a slatted wood-gated stairway. The connection with the elements and nature is clear: inescapably in touch with the natural world, it is an open platform with the four-poster bed almost abutting the tree trunk and just a gauzy mosquito net covering. Dinner is served at sunset in some style at a rustic wooden table set out on the deck and lit with flickering oil lamps.

A ship's crow's nest may seem an odd comparison in such a parched landscape, but the two-tiered platform really does feel like a lonely lookout point from which to survey the rolling grasslands below. Look up, and you'll be engulfed by the blue waves of sky and an overwhelming sense of how small and insignificant you are in this hostile landscape.

style notes for the kingston treehouse

For those of us who like their lions, elephants, buffalo, leopards and rhinos a little more removed from their four-poster bed, there's a second treehouse called Kingston, which is more contained with glass walls and a slatted roof. Instead of a door to prevent animal ingress, this treehouse is secured by its own drawbridge.

By day, sunlight sears through the crude criss-cross thatching but as evening draws in, the space is suffused with a dream-like pinky glow, warming the contemporary decor and injecting romance. On the smaller, lower-decked terrace area are cushioned armchairs which are the natural vantage point for watching the sky plunge from dramatic reds to inky blackness. It is lit by oil lanterns and supplies are delivered to you in the form of a picnic. You then climb into bed under the mosquito net and fall asleep under a canopy of stars.

Although 'interior' doesn't adquately describe the open outdoor nature of this place, the furnishings are appropriately understated in hues of grey, white, black and purple, along with the untreated timber of the beams and bed. The touches of luxury have a similar effect of paring down the rawness of the space. The furniture is, at first glance, unassuming so nothing detracts from the scenes playing out on the plains. Look closer, though, and you'll appreciate how considered every piece and its positioning is. There is real craftsmanship on show here.

living room

In a remote valley filled with oak trees in the heart of the Welsh mountains, an area recognised by UNESCO as a biosphere, Peter Canham has created some unique treehouses. Each one has its own name and was constructed according to the best ecological building principles, using local materials and influenced by natural forms of architecture.

The construction was guided by the natural form of the oak trees and sensible aerodynamic considerations in this windy valley. The natural formed shapes are best when the wind blows and, in Peter's words, 'The treehouses are on floating joints so that when the trees sway, the buildings stay still. We build them with locally sourced bone oak, larch, Scots pine and cedar. They have low-impact floating joints to sway gently with the breeze.'

These treehouses are designed to be off-grid (not reliant on mains utilities) and their occupants enjoy a self-sufficient lifestyle, gently nudged into tune with their environment. Each architecturally ovoid and fluid form, with its peaked overhanging roof, wide central doorway and two huge eye-like circular windows, expresses the 'living' nature of the structure. It's thick and sturdy, without being overwhelming – the features and natural forms are delicate and crafted. You feel as though you could escape from the outside world and hibernate. There's no phone, no electricity, no Wi-Fi. You are lulled into embracing this alternative lifestyle as you are forced to use your imagination, unwind and become aware of your basic needs – chopping wood for warmth and seeking shelter from the elements. In this immensely beautiful space, you can appreciate the achievement of being resourceful and sustaining yourself physically.

style notes for gwdy hw

'Gwdy Hw', a Welsh name for 'owl' used by children, is a treehouse set in a larch tree 10m (35ft) above the ground. Larch is a springy and flexible tree, so you can feel the movement within as the wind blows and the tree swings. Designed for couples, the main door of the treehouse opens into a two-chamber house with a leaf-stencilled arch leading from the living area to a fluffy pillow-strewn bedroom. Decorated sensitively throughout with an eye for detail, the house gives a firm nod to Welsh traditional design, with solid wooden bespoke furniture. The interiors use rounded natural forms – they are artistic but not elaborate and overworked, and even the kettle has a soft, modular outline. Evoking memories of flapjack making, the light fittings have been fashioned from empty golden syrup tins and cast a delicate shimmering accent against the wooden surfaces.

A separate willow enclosure at ground level houses the shower. It is operated by a simple pulley and the log-burning stove in the treehouse produces steaming hot water. In winter the route to the shower is enhanced by walking on the crisp frosty ground. At night, the sun dips below the horizon, turning the forest red, and the trees are dappled with silver in the moonlight. Even reaching the treehouse is part of the experience and the rope knots on the spiral stairway are trimmed with coppiced hazel – both beautiful and practical. This is one of those rare places where man, nature and a sustainable life can coexist comfortably.

style notes for pen y bryn

The name 'Pen y bryn' means 'head of the hill' in Welsh and, indeed, the treehouse stands on a remote hilltop 305m (1,000ft) above the Dyfi valley. A large treehouse built into an oak tree, it was designed for families with a sense of adventure. Access is by foot only, with your belongings hauled across a stream and up a steep forest bank in a handmade cart. Once inside, you're sheltered from the elements but not isolated from them, the stable oak tree creaking like a ship in the wind.

A wood-burning stove heats the highly insulated space and the spring water for the shower is stored in a separate coppiced hazel structure at ground level. The compost toilet is located in a smaller adjacent build in the tree, accessed by a wobbly rope bridge. Gaslight or candles illuminate this arboreal world, creating a stagelike atmosphere of flickering shadows. The oak interior is built to last. You can access this magical world up in the trees via a wooden spiral staircase, clinging around a gnarled trunk, and leading over a chain and rope bridge to the fixed deck outside the house.

This isn't so much an escape from the real world as an invitation into it. The rules are off-grid and you have to participate and live within these parameters. However, the experience is not uncomfortable or harsh, and there is a satisfying fusion of aesthetics and the sustainable. A sense of calm and tranquillity permeates this unique space.

rhino plains camp

The pioneer spirit still lives on and is evident in this safari camp and treehouse retreat on a 120sq km (46sq mile) private concession within the Kruger Reserve in South Africa. This is a place that has retained a sense of adventure and authenticity – it hasn't lost touch with its past. It is simple and treads lightly on the environment, sited around a campfire and a small plunge pool. The earth-toned treetop safari tents, raised on poles above the ground, are made from traditional canvas and wood and they sit within an acacia knob thorn thicket.

Coming here you feel like an intrepid naturalist; this is close to nature and about as close as it gets. All you need do is to just pack a few clothes and provisions in a rucksack and make the two-hour hike away from the main camp to the treehouses, which are simple sleeping platform structures, built around a watering hole. Supported by stilts, they offer an alternative encounter with nature in the open air with the minimum of shelter. At night you can lie and listen to the hyenas cackle and the elephants roar, but your feet are safely off the ground, the stars and Milky Way lighting up the sky above you.

Erecting your own mosquito net, a flysheet if necessary, and making your own bed are all part of this experience – unpacking your simple belongings, you take part, engage and live the dream. There's no internet, no mains services – just paraffin lamps and a dinner cooked over a camp fire. It's all about you, the elements and the incredible natural world around you.

style notes

Colonial life is from another time, but colonial style still has a resonance and credibility in terms of its simple classic design and use of high-quality materials. These treehouse tents embody practical and functional luxury: polished teak, light olive safari canvas, sturdy wooden tent posts and guy ropes, brass hooks and even a silver coffee pot – glinting touches against the muted tones of the olive greens and browns. Evocative of a colonial outpost, the tents are furnished in a way that modern glamping strives to imitate. Their thick sturdy furniture and comfortable mattresses are welcoming, the sheets are crisp white linen and there are flashes of luxury where it's deemed necessary.

The tents are strong with raw unfinished wooden beams, providing a contrast with the more finished floorboards and rougher supporting pillars. The showers are built around the natural bark of a tree trunk, the shiny brass hooks sitting easily alongside the roughly hewn supports – it's a place of contrasting materials and textures, each with its own honesty and a story. And stripping this back even further, the treehouses provide the bare necessities of shelter without even a nod to the hi-tech world – you really are just out there. This is no twee colonial theme park – you are back in the wilderness and part of the wild world.

The Alnwick Garden Treehouse restaurant, shop and treetop walkway were commissioned to enhance the acclaimed gardens created by Jacques Wirtz. The brief to Napper Architects was to create an archetypal treehouse with an organic feel within an area of mature lime trees without damaging their root systems. To strengthen the huge 550sq m (5,920sq ft) build, a supporting structure was built beneath the trees to allow the building to move with them. This was an enormous enterprise: 14 pile cap foundations had to be randomly positioned at a depth of 12m (39ft) away from the major tree root system. On top of the piles, Douglas fir struts were used to support a 'tabletop' structure of Siberian larch beams, selected for their length and strength, with a yellow Balau hardwood decking on top of which the main building sits.

The technical challenges were vast yet, in spite of the precise construction, the architects wanted the finished appearance to be organic and natural. Creating this look would be no easy task, so to differentiate between areas of cladding, wonky joints and handmade character details they also produced hand-drawn coloured elevations and perspectives to convey a naturalistic finish to the skilled craftsmen inclined towards meticulous, detailed perfection.

The trees grow up through the building of the main restaurant structure. Hemp rope is wound around the junction of the deck and the trunks to allow for movement during high winds. Technically and creatively challenging, this inspirational treehouse successfully combines practical and fantastical elements that can be extracted and condensed for more modest builds. You cannot but admire its scale. It's glorious.

the alnwick garden treehouse

style notes

Set among the trees rather than being supported by them, this treehouse engages with their branches and trunks and transports you into a magical experience. The buttressing pillars sprout out, angular like the branches of the trees, and the whole structure feels as though it's moving – almost bouncing off the pillars. Even though it's huge, it feels light and gives you the impression of being on a moving rather than a static structure, like the rope bridges, which are dynamic and free.

The hands of the skilled designers, engineers and craftsmen are only lightly visible. Technology is cleverly cloaked in nature – the materials are carefully chosen and a huge amount of effort has gone into making the treehouse, inside and out, look handcrafted, as if it were part of a mysterious organic process rather than a carefully designed and executed building project.

In its design it is delightfully quirky – higgledy-piggledy and a patchwork of different textures, materials and angles. It's a magical childlike retreat with the

tree trunks piercing the structure and branches cascading into the interior, where a wood-burning fire magically glows. Fortunately, building controls permitted the installation of the open log fire in the restaurant. Its position was dictated by the location of the insulated flue, which discharges out above the canopy of the adjacent trees. The exterior tone and essence carry through into the interior: even the varied height chair backs with cut-outs look as if they could have been carved by elves, and folkloric themes and architecture cover every inch. Harsh reality is kept out – this is a whimsical, playful and sweet space.

Along with the creative garden designer Jacques Wirtz, the architects and the Duchess of Northumberland have created an arboreal world – an imaginative and alternative reality. As well as the treehouse, there's an extensive deck area housing a bar, and a three-sided partially covered raised walkway through the trees with two suspension bridges. You need an extraordinary level of ambition, vision, conception, build and finish for such an idea to be successful. Here it's amazing.

Here in Nashville, Tennessee, music, creativity and the entrepreneurial spirit run deep. This treehouse restaurant represents each of these elements, which are shared between the owners and creators of this unique space. Apart from the crafted multi-coloured, wood-painted treehouse carrying the neon sign, the structure is symbolic rather than practical. It's off limits to the diners because it's structurally unable to support a potential crush of people. Sandwiched onto the main body of the building, an outpost and lovingly crafted lighthouse, it's built from recycled timbers raised above the ground on small stilts.

The house was previously owned by Buddy Spicher, a legendary fiddle player. During his 25-year tenure he constructed the treehouse in his backyard for his kids and grandchildren to play in with a music studio in the house nextdoor. When he moved out, his son Matt, together with extended family members and friends, pooled their talents, labour and energies to create a restaurant. The treehouse stayed and the living space in the house was converted into a dining area, taking care along the way to salvage and reuse as many of the original materials as possible. The front of the bar was made from the old doors while the original door knobs are now used as hooks for hanging handbags. The old timbers were removed and re-milled to create tables and chairs, so nothing that could be recycled has been wasted.

The original treehouse consisted of just the top section but, over the years, Buddy and his family added to it and during the restaurant transformation it was enlarged and extended outwards over the other tree limbs and beyond to make it a local landmark.

nashville treehouse restaurant

style notes
Reusing existing materials helped to make this a passion-led project – a celebration of life. The design is not something that has been imported or transposed from a magazine image. Instead, it has evolved organically from the building's history, resonating with echoes and musical notes of the past, the new and the old sitting happily together side by side. The result is a comfortable interior: the rusticity is countered by good design and a well-organised professional kitchen.

Along with the inevitable Nashville vibe, warehouse-style features characterise this space where wood is the major element. It is well worn, textured, weathered, grooved, ingrained, etched with history and resilience, painted and distressed. It's a handcrafted triumph of beauty, with dazzling colours, textures and confidence. Raw, simple and unadorned strings of festoon lighting, with the warm gold filament of the bulbs, criss-cross the space, hinting at a party or impromptu gathering.

modern

Sometimes it is difficult to develop a design idea much beyond the drawing board or initial working model. Here, however, the treehouse concept has been picked up and shaken, stripped of its rustic, ramshackle inheritance, and transformed into a vehicle for an innovative and fresh design. These treehouses engage with the ground, the branches and the elements – and they look amazing, too. No wonder rock stars and design aficionados love them! You probably will, too.

Delve even deeper into the following pages and look beyond the visual – these show-stopping treehouses really are jaw-dropping creations while embodying everything that is brave and unique. They lift and encourage you with all sorts of possibilities: technically and stylistically as well thanks to their their downright beauty. With designs that allude to nature, including birdhouses, cocoons and wasps' nests, their inspiration is widely sourced and referenced. With so much drama and beauty it's easy to overlook their technical brilliance.

Dustin Feider's O2 treehouses, with their geodesic forms and architectural internal spaces, are hybrids of nature and technology. Likewise, the witty Bird Apartment in Japan seeks to engage its human occupant with the natural world, creating a space in which birds and humans live side by side. On a Spanish island, a simple grooming retreat built on stilts becomes a haven of relaxation and solace for riders and their horses. And almost invisible amongst the trees in a remote area of southwest England is an unusual woodland office that is home to an architectural practice. All these treehouses are a living testimony to their designers' and owners' ingenuity and resourcefulness in pursuing their dreams and turning them into reality.

O2 treehouses

Using geodesic forms and cocoonish environments, these beautiful tree-strung structures were designed to recreate the experience of a road trip. Up off the ground, separated from the solidity of the real world, they are the ultimate release. These fresh interpretations of treehouses were created with the traditional intention of providing inspiring spaces for people.

Dustin Feider was inspired by the American architect and inventor Buckminster Fuller and his unusual approach to design. He loved being outdoors and creating small spaces and environments that integrated with the natural world. To find the best form and structure in this context, he kept searching for the perfect shape. For him, the design process started by sitting up in a tree, imaging the forms that might work in a sketchbook. Through a combination of thumbnail rough sketches and budgetary and technical considerations, his plans gradually took shape. He relishes new challenges and an innate curiosity informs and fuels his work.

Creating these structures requires specialist expertise and competence, and even though Dustin has some knowledge of engineering, components and load-bearing, he works with a structural engineer in the technical aspects of the design and construction process, including calculating the load, determining how much pressure can be asserted on a tree, specifying the positioning of the fixing bolts and aligning practical and structural elements with the aesthetic.

The interiors are treated as architectural spaces – they have been designed to feel light and expansive. The sphere is seen more as a 'vessel' with the ambience of a gallery space.

The idea behind this is to encourage people to discover the environment and experience 'the animated canopy completely surrounding them'. Back in the studio where he builds the structures, Dustin is fascinated by the perfect sphere. He works thematically with the inspirational geodesic form and appreciates the transformational qualities and aesthetics of different materials. For him, there is so much to be explored.

style notes for the copper nest treehouse

This treehouse structure was created as the ultimate backyard party pad for a client in Wisconsin, and there is something mysterious and monumental about it. It is cinematic yet timeless, something which the forest has grown up around, shrouding it in mystery. It was designed ambitiously as a party space to accommodate up to 200 people and is the epitome of rock 'n' roll. The plan was that a small number of guests should feel just as comfortable and at home in the treehouse as a large crowd. You reach the treehouse via the 8m (27ft) gently stepped side entry pathway that links it to the backyard decking below. A subtly painted line down the middle of the path leads the eye, directing you on your journey. The treehouse, created from cedar, steel and reclaimed wood, is geodesic in form with the facade enhanced with the addition of 45 steel, wedge-shaped canopies. To complement the wooded landscape, each canopy is given a rust patina in tones of rich burnt umber and reddish gold to enhance the sense of a weathered bucolic aesthetic.

style notes for the healdsburg treehouse

Clinging, wrapping and engaging fully with its host tree, the Healdsburg treehouse, which was designed for a private client in California, brought with it a whole new level of complexity in its design and production challenges. Dustin wanted to create a structure that really responded to the tree and fitted within the branches with a new degree of engagement. Its naturalistic appearance belies the effort, thought and work that went into achieving this incredible form. Using a laser scan and a working model of the tree, the structure evolved, utilising reclaimed Douglas fir timbers and 34 gauge steel for the exterior, with high-density polypropylene panels. The interior flooring is hardwood. This treehouse has a distinctive organic feel, which is intricate, unified, light, complex and cohesive – it's a beautiful hybrid of nature and technology and a harmonious piece of architecture.

style notes for the honey sphere

Truly a rock star's treehouse, this was built for Robby Krieger, the guitarist in the Doors, in his Beverly Hills backyard. Robby wanted somewhere to relax, feel immersed in nature, watch the wildlife and, of course, play his guitar. Dustin had already built a treehouse on the same street and such was its appeal that other neighbours commissioned them, too, making it 'treehouse alley'. Honey Sphere was born from all the good vibrations in Beverly Hills. Built in redwood with a steel floor, the 6m (20ft) diameter structure was modelled first, the challenge being to ensure an exact fit between its many facets. It needed to be millimetre perfect to accommodate entry and exit points for 12 branches and, as Dustin says, 'fighting gravity was difficult'. Piece by piece, the structure was assembled in the tree and was constantly pulled up and joined until eventually all the pieces, 210 of them with 420 facets, were bolted together. And when the final piece of this massive 3D jigsaw was hauled into place, it fitted exactly.

The supporting tree is an oak and care was taken to ensure that its beauty could be enjoyed by future generations. Its upper branches contribute to carrying the load by gently supporting the sphere by means of steel cabling. Using leftover wood from the sphere construction, the interior floor was created, adding a mandala print, and it is secured around the tree trunk with a steel girdle. Robby uses the sphere to hang out with friends and to create music, often riffing there on his acoustic 12-string guitar. He thinks it lends a magical feeling to its occupants, sparking the imaginations of everyone who enters.

style notes for the leaf house

Luminous like a gigantic full moon in a tree top, the Leaf House's light shone so brightly that some neighbours asked for it to be turned off! This was back in 2005 and it was the first of Dustin's commissions, an outpouring of youthful optimism and energy that was more like a prototype. He constructed it single-handedly in his garage and installed it on his own.

Built with aluminium struts and an interior canopy of high-density translucent polypropylene panels, it measures 4m (13ft) in diameter and uses recycled plastic for the flooring and basket lift. It is built around the joints of the tree trunk and branches and held tight at a terrifying 15m (50ft) off the ground – the highest treehouse Dustin has built. Like a glowing orb, Chinese lantern or escaped balloon drifting into the sky and caught in a tree, it casts a striking silhouette, drawing your eye and lifting the spirit. It is intriguing – part treehouse, part sculpture, part spaceship – ready to leave its treetop tether and float off on an adventure.

This was designed as a bird multi-occupancy 'apartment building' and one-person treehouse. **bird apartment**
The commonality is an adjoining wall drilled with 78 tiny holes, which results in a unique,
experiential birdhouse cum peep show – a conceptual piece brought into reality. The aim was
to capture the small but amazing moments in life that we appreciate but don't linger over.
This treehouse promotes and increases our access to and interest in the natural world. Here
the birds clearly take precedence over the humans; we are just visitors, spectators and an
audience. The designers describe it as 'collective housing for many birds and one person'.

Sited in a forest in Komoro City in the Nagano Prefecture in Japan, the treehouse was
designed by Nendo for the Ando Momofuku Foundation. On the front of the structure there
are 78 nesting boxes, similar in form but varying in size, and on the other face there's just one
entry hole to a single chamber, enabling the human occupant to peek through tiny holes into
each of the birdhouses. To gain access to the treehouse, you have to climb a ladder and crawl
through the round entrance way. Once inside, you can stand under the apex roof and peer into
the individual 'houses' on the 'bird' side of the apartment.

Intended to induce an emotional reaction and engagement, the design of the 'human house'
is a scaled-up version of the smaller and numerous birdhouses. The circular entrance, colour
and simple apex roofline mimic the classic birdbox design on the front of the apartment,
tessellated together in a repeating but varied form. The implication is that birds are of equal
consideration and value and are worthy of our attention.

style notes

This stunning piece of simple, clean-lined modern design is as playful and witty as it is beautiful and mysterious. Looking out of the round window, you momentarily become a bird, sharing the same view of interlacing branches framed by the circle.

At first glance, the minimalist wooden structure appears to be painted principally in white – but look more closely, and you can make out numerous other tones. The muted white, grey and green strips that clad the exterior subtly blend into the palette of the sky and branches, making the house almost disappear into the surrounding forest. Moreover, each birdhouse has its own individual colour, ranging from white to very pale grey. The design is simple and clean-lined, the outer shape mimicking the repeated shape of the component birdhouses, with their differing rooflines creating a zigzag relief.

This treehouse contrives to be fragile but also quietly grand; it's monumental, a wonderfully conceived piece of design. There is something pleasing to the human eye about this familiar shape. We like and take comfort from buildings shaped like this. Quiet and unobtrusive, it uses repetition and seemingly simple design with consideration, cleverly combining the individual spaces to create the whole, which is as beautiful as each individual nesting box.

This charming, poetic structure makes the universal appeal of treehouses explicit: the physical ability to leave the ground, create an escape and provide a fresh environment and an opportunity to be different. The tall entrance ladder conveys the sense of the journey up into the tree, away from the human world into the fascinating territory of birds and aerial life.

This unique and aesthetically simple retreat is built on stilts and focuses on the conceptual and practical functions of a restful place of solace for horses as well as riders. The project evolved when the owner left city life behind and returned to Mallorca, Spain, to manage her family's agricultural business. The design, function and purpose of the build were inspired by the routine of grooming before and after riding. This is valuable and reassuring for both the animal and rider, and the owner believes that the mind and spirit as well as the body are nurtured by the acts of grooming, drinking and resting.

The location in the centre of a barley field surrounded by wild olive trees has distant sea views, and the build is composed of two structures, both of which are elevated on timber stilts. The smaller one, a criss-cross wooden frame, is for tethering horses and holds a squared-off conical water tank and feeding trough. The main structure, which measures 3m x 3m (9ft 10in x 9ft 10in), is designed for contemplation in a sealed-off, inward-looking hut. With an open top and translucent side walls, it allows a softer, more gentle light to penetrate and provide a panoramic yet muted visual experience of the landscape.

Linking the two structures is a narrow elevated wooden walkway, which slices through the rippling barley – two straight lines that meet at a gentle angle. The journey along this path continues up a ladder, enabling the owner to climb into the retreat through a hatch. Internally the space is subdivided by screens of white mosquito netting, creating softly differing areas with diffuse opacities of light and degrees of engagement or introspection.

the grooming retreat

style notes

Cinematic in style and emanating a sense of the 'other-worldly', this magical interpretation of a practical grooming retreat is almost invisible, like an oasis shimmering in the desert. Beautifully designed but also poetic and quietly monumental, the structures are in harmony with the landscape – light and textural rather than presenting a bulky or dense presence.

The thick barley field, the thin blue slither of sea on the horizon, the location and its component parts each play an important role in the design as a whole. While it is sturdy and strong, it evokes a sense of something ephemeral, fragile and delicate – the sky is a constant presence, filtering through the criss-crossing timber elevation and fine mosquito mesh.

The interior has appropriately simple leggy furniture – a stool and small slatted-topped table – with some dried grasses in an old clear glass wine bottle, baskets, a Victorian dressing stand-style washing bowl and a mirror. They are essential and decorative items that possess the qualities of space, light and nature. There are no painted surfaces, only earth tones that have been incorporated where the material is unadorned, rustic and simple. The pieces have been chosen so as not to distract or detract from the structure's purpose.

This is an intriguing space, both utterly modest and complex, created with the highest conceptual reasoning yet glamorous and inspirational. Its use of materials is exemplary and it represents the creative and restorative properties of being raised just a few feet off the ground and having a breezy, soft and translucent filter on the earthly world below.

woodland office

How do you build an office for an architectural practice that prides itself on doing things differently? By siting it in woodland and employing a team of untrained family and friends to construct it. Such was the unconventional genesis of Invisible Studio's new headquarters near Bath in southwest England, a 55sq m (592sq ft) enclosed space accessed via a bridge from a slope flanking one side. Below is an open workshop for making full-scale models.

Nobody who worked on the project had constructed a building before. It was an exercise in establishing a system of building that could be built by unskilled labour, with only minimal drawings, allowing ad hoc improvisation and escaping the tyranny of predetermined design. The finished project looks unorthodox, but for a building that was constructed without much discernible forethought, it's delightfully in tune with its surroundings, which provided the basic materials for the construction. All the untreated, unseasoned timber was grown and milled on site. Some of the trees even yielded the scaffolding while the office was being assembled, before ultimately being repurposed to form the bridge and floor. Continuing this trend, even the heating comes from waste wood from the forest.

The treehouse more than pays its debt to its environment: rainwater is diverted from the roof to a nearby pond, while the footings (mixed by hand) were designed to be as minimally invasive as possible. In a further nod to environmental concerns, recycled materials were used when possible, from the windows (scavenged from a skip) and floor paint (the leftovers from another project) to the carefully patchworked offcuts of insulation in the walls.

style notes

Imagination, a resourceful use of recycled materials and a workforce trained on the job are a force to be reckoned with, as this strikingly beautiful treehouse proves. The striated exterior is the first of many exquisite surprises. It is formed from oriented strand board (OSB), which has been painted with a black waterproof coating. On top of it the team layered horizontal stripes of untreated timber that will age to a skeletal grey colour over time. They provide a reassuringly solid rib cage around this living, breathing piece of architecture.

For mastermind Piers Taylor, the treehouse is designed 'to settle down into the landscape and evolve over time'. The long walkway serves as a reminder of this journey, weaving over the woodland floor. From the start of the path, the treehouse is almost completely camouflaged – a credit to its sustainable, low-impact design, allowing it to be woven into the forest setting. The interior is equally earthy. The warm red tones of the floor provide a natural contrast to the lime green of the leaves outside. Blue chairs give a welcome daub of colour, a clever reminder of the sky that's obscured by the canopy of the trees above and the corrugated Perspex window surrounds, which blur the outline between the organised workspace and untamed nature.

Amid all these careful colours, the silver glint of insulation behind the unclad walls is a jolting reminder that this isn't some primitive hut of yore but a twenty-first century example of architectural experimentation. When darts of sunlight catch the foil, they inject just the right amount of razzle-dazzle into this otherwise chameleon-like cabin.

sourcebook

architects

**AANDEBOOM/Rogier Martens
& Sam van Veluw**
DIY treehouse
www.aandeboom.nl

Christopher Smith, Architect
the tree room (Tree Room, 2009)
www.csmitharchitect.com

Griffin Collier
the lau treehouse
www.griffincollier.com

H&P Architects/HPA
blooming bamboo home
www.hpa.vn

Invisible Studio
woodland office
www.invisiblestudio.org

Nendo
bird apartment
www.nendo.jp

Nicko Elliot
modern backyard treehouse
www.civilianprojects.com

**Prentis Hale
SHED Architecture + Design**
treehouse home
www.shedbuilt.com

**Rockefeller Partners
Architects**
LA modern
www.rockefeller-pa.com

Tate Harmer
dartmoor cocoon treehouse

artists

artist's fruitcrate treehouse
Leonard van Munster
www.leonardvanmunster.com

caravan in the sky
Benedetto Bufalino
www.benedettobufalino.com

gallery treehouse
Andrew Shirley & Amanda Wong
Artists/Curatorial Collaborative:
Andreas Greiner, Lydia Wilhelm,
Reto Steiner, Stefanie & Maureen
Kagi

london chill-out treehouse
Keren Luchtenstein
kerenluchtenstein@gmail.com
William McLellan
willy@willysmax.com

craftspeople

gallery treehouse
Mike O'Toole

the grooming retreat
Chief carpenters: Sindre Sahlqvist Blakar,
Eirik Stormo
Hands-on collaborators: Marie Monsen, Julie
Hauge, Suchi Vora, Martin Plante, Nataliya
Kuznetsova

living room
Bespoke Woodland Furniture: Merlin's Craft
max@merlins-craft.co.uk
tel: 07856 924675
Sutton Creative – Artisan Woodworking and
Stonework
tel: 07936 455784
Build team: Peter Canham (project manager),
Louis Sutton, Max Jenkins, Dylan Matthews,
Mark Bond

designers

brazilian beachfront treehouse
www.thenovogratz.com

brooklyn backyard treehouse
Alexandra Meyn
www.alexandrameyn.com

canopy staircase
Thorwald ter Kulve
www.thorterkulve.com
Robert Featherstone MacIntyre
www.studiomcintyre.com

frugal modernism
www.modfrugal.com

the grooming retreat
www.gartnerfuglen.com
www.marianadelas.com

O2 treehouses
Dustin Feider
www.o2treehouse.com

primrose hill treehouse
film production designer John Beard
www.jbeard.info/

sauna treehouse
Duilio Forte
www.atelierforte.com

todd oldham's treehouse
www.toddoldhamstudio.com

utah leather worker's treehouse
Quinn Peterson QP Collections
www.qpcollections.com

places to visit

the alnwick garden treehouse
The Alnwick Garden & The Alnwick
Garden Treehouse
www.alnwickgarden.com

amid the lavender fields
La Piantata, Arlena di Castro, Italy
www.lapiantata.it

living room
www.living-room.co

nashville treehouse restaurant
The Treehouse Restaurant, 1011 Clearview
Ave, Nashville, TN 37206
www.treehousenashville.com

rhino plains camp
Plains Camp Kruger National Park,
Skukuza 1350, South Africa

safari treehouses
Lion Sands Game Reserve
www.lionsands.com

sparrow house
www.outlandishholidays.co.uk

tudor treehouse
www.PitchfordEstate.com

tuscan treehouse
www.airbnb.com/rooms/1621152

suppliers

the lau treehouse
Hadco Metals
www.hadco-metal.com
Hull Forest Products
www.hullforest.com
Lindapter
www.lindapter.com
Mid City Stee
www.midcitysteel.com
Treehouse Supplies
www.treehousesupplies.com
Yarde Metals
www.yarde.com

living room
Interior design: Camilla Norberg,
The Deco Shop
www.deco-shop.co.uk
tel: 01654 7000001

utah leather worker's treehouse
Treasures Antique Mall
www.treasuresantiquemall.blogspot

credits

We would like to thank all the treehouse owners for allowing us to photograph their 'cool treehouses':

The Alnwick Garden & The Alnwick Garden Treehouse www.alnwickgarden.com

Riccardo Barthel www.riccardobarthel.it/en/ www.airbnb.com/rooms/1621152

John Beard http://www.jbeard.info

Mark Bond and Peter Canham, Living Room Experiences Ltd www.living-room.co

Griffin Collier, plus the Kickstarter backers, the Treehouse team, and everyone involved in the design and construction of this structure iwht a special thank you to the project's patrons, Vlaire Woo and Gordon Lau

Dustin Feider www.o2treehouse.com

Duilio Forte, AtelierFORTE www.atelierforte.com

Gartnerfuglen (www.gartnerfuglen.com) & Mariana de Delás (www.marianadelas.com)

Prentis Hale SHED Architecture + Design www.shedbuilt.com

Invisible Studio Architects www.invisiblestudio.org

Thorwald ter Kulve and Robert McIntyre ww.canopystair.com

Chrislyn Lawrence www.chrislynlawrence.com

Lion Sands Game Reserve www.lionsands.com

Plains Camp, Kruger National Park, Skukuza 1350, South Africa

Rogier Martens & Sam van Veluw www.aandeboom.nl

William McLellan and Keren Luchtenstein willy@willysmax.com
kerenluchtenstein@gmail.com

Jonathan Melville-Smith www.outlandishholidays.co.uk

Alexandra Meyn www.alexandrameyn.com

Leonard van Munster www.Leonardvanmunster.com

Rowena & James Nason www.pitchfordestate.com

www.thenovogratz.com

www.toddoldham.com

Quinn Peterson www.qpcollections.com
The Treehouse Restaurant, 1011 Clearview Ave, Nashville, TN 37206
www.treehousenashville.com

Amanda Wong and Andrew H. Shirley

**All photography by Tina Hillier unless otherwise stated.
www.tinahillier.com**

Endpapers	Photography: Jane Field-Lewis; artwork: Heather Pollington
Page 1	Dick Duyves website indien mogelijk www.duyves.com
Pages 2–3	Heath Raymond Photography
Pages 6–9	Dustin Feider www.o2treehouse.com
Pages 12–13	Barbara Zonzin www.barbarazonzin.com
Pages 14–15	Jesse Colin Jackson www.jessecolinjackson.com
Pages 20–21	Christopher Smith, Architect www.csmitharchitect.com
Pages 22–23	Tony McIntyre www.tonymcintyre.com
Page 24	Griffin Collier www.griffincollier.com
Pages 26–29	Doan Thanh Ha, H&P Architects I HPA www.hpa.vn
Pages 30–33	Eric Staudenmaier Photography www.ericstaudenmaier.com
Pages 34–35	Griffin Collier www.griffincollier.com
Pages 36–41	Mark Woods Photography www.mwoodsphoto.com
Pages 42–43	Danielle Acken, DL ACKEN PHOTOGRAPHY www.dlackenphotography.com
Pages 56–59	Richard Powers richard@richardpowers.co.uk
Pages 60–63	Ariadna Bufi/ The Novogratz
Page 68	Michael Smallcombe
Page 70	Deneka Peniston www.penistonphotography.com
Pages 70–71	© Trevor Tondro / *The New York Times* / Redux / eyevine
Pages 72–73	Michael Smallcombe
Pages 74–75	Duilio Forte, AtelierFORTE www.atelierforte.com
Page 76	Benedetto Bufalino www.benedettobufalino.com
Pages 78–79	Dick Duyves www.duyves.com & Leonard Van Munster www.leonardvanmunster.com
Pages 80–81	Benedetto Bufalino www.benedettobufalino.com
Pages 82–83	Amanda Wong; Andrew H; Shirley; Luna Park The Street Spot www.thestreetspot.com
Page 86	Quinn Peterson www.qpcollections.com
Pages 88–89	modfrugal www.modfrugal.com
Pages 100–105	Quinn Peterson www.qpcollections.com
Page 106	Chrislyn Lawrence www.chrislynlawrence.com
Page 134	nendo www.nendo.jp
Pages 136–137	Dustin Feider www.o2treehouse.com
Pages 138–139	Benjamin Ariff www.benjaminariff.com
Pages 140–143	Dustin Feider www.o2treehouse.com
Pages 148–151	Gartnerfuglen www.gartnerfuglen.com & Mariana de Delás www.marianadelas.com
Pages 152–155	Piers Taylor, Invisible Studio www.invisiblestudio.org; Andy Matthews www.andymatthewsphoto.com

acknowledgements

Writing and art directing the *my cool...* books is a privilege that opens up whole new worlds of the creative and enterprising endeavours of others. It is a pleasure to be able to dip into and share with you the talent and courage that each of these projects and their creators brings. In the process of writing and photographing this book and visiting the treehouses, I have been made to feel welcome, seen nature from a different point of view and not only had some close calls with both the elements and the wildlife but also an enormous amount of fun, experiences for which I am very grateful.

I'd like to thank the team at Pavilion, especially Fiona Holman who brings good guidance, experience and wisdom to these projects, Kom in marketing, Laura in the design deparment, and the hands-on design skills of the talented and ever-amusing Steve Russell. These are not single-handed projects and I appreciate the skills, opinions and talents of the people in my own team: Emily Lutyens, Heather Thomas, Sarah Henshaw and Sarah Riley. And, last but not least, I am grateful to the photographer Tina Hillier for her inspiring images. Thank you all.

The ongoing success of the books, each with their quirky and creative subject matter, makes clear to me every single day that there is great beauty and joy out there. Whether these projects cost a fortune or very little is immaterial. Being able to share them with you is what matters. I hope you enjoy them and feel inspired, too.

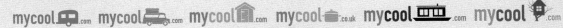

Jane Field-Lewis

Jane Field-Lewis is a stylist for film, photography and TV and is also the creative consultant behind the hit C4 series *Amazing Spaces*. Her work is truly global – both her styling work and books are internationally successful. She has written and art directed *my cool caravan*, *my cool campervan*, and *my cool shed*, and co-authored with the television presenter George Clarke the books to accompany the *Amazing Spaces* TV series, which was BAFTA nominated in 2015.

She has an enduring love for people and style, believing that the two are closely entwined. Her career is based on the aesthetic, whether high- or low-style, and across people and objects.

With her styling work, *Amazing Spaces* and *my cool...* she hopes to inspire an affordable, individual and creative approach to any project.

Additional captions: page 1 artist's fruitcrate treehouse; pages 2–3 'Room with a View'; page 4 living room (Gwdy Hw); page 6 02 treehouses/honey sphere ; page 9 02 treehouses/copper nest; pages 10–11 primrose hill treehouse; pages 24–25 the lau treehouse; pages 44–45 amid the lavender fields/the black cabin; pages 68–69 dartmoor cocoon treehouse; pages 76–77 caravan in the sky; pages 86–87 utah leather worker's treehouse; pages 106–107 the treehouse restaurant; pages 134–135 bird apartment; page 160 rhino plains camp

First published in the United Kingdom in 2016 by
Pavilion
1 Gower Street
London WC1E 6HD

Copyright © 2016 Pavilion Books Company Ltd
Text copyright © 2016 Jane Field-Lewis

my cool® is the registered trademark of Jane Field
(UK TM registration no. 2575447).

Editorial Director Fiona Holman
Styling by Jane Field-Lewis
Editor Heather Thomas

Photography by Tina Hillier
Design Steve Russell

This book can be ordered direct from the publisher at
www.pavilionbooks.com

ISBN 978-1-910-49618-3

A CIP catalogue record for this book is available from the British Library.

10 9 8 7 6 5 4 3 2 1

Reproduction by Mission, Hong Kong
Printed and bound by Toppan Leefung Printing Ltd, China